Teaching History
With Film and Television

JOHN E. O'CONNOR

2

DISCUSSIONS ON TEACHING

AMERICAN HISTORICAL ASSOCIATION

400 A Street, SE, Washington, D.C. 20003

JOHN E. O'CONNOR is a professor of history at New Jersey Institute of Technology, chairman of the Historians Film Committee, and editor of its quarterly journal *Film & History*. He has written and edited several books on early American history and in the historical study of film and television. He also designed the NEH-funded project "The Historian and the Moving-Image Media," and has directed this project for the American Historical Association. He wishes to thank the other participants in the project for their assistance in developing the ideas presented here. Contributions from twelve of them will be published in a forthcoming book entitled *Image as Artifact: The Historical Analysis of Film and Television*.

This book replaces Teaching History with Film *(1974) by John E. O'Connor and Martin A. Jackson in the* Discussions on Teaching *series. It is a completely new work that reflects the most up-to-date information available on the subject.*

Part of a larger project funded by the National Endowment for the Humanities

AHA Staff Editor: MAUREEN VINCENT-MORGAN

1988.

Library of Congress catalog card number: 87-72569
ISBN: 0-87229-040-9
Printed in the United States of America

CONTENTS

Teaching History
With Film and Television

JOHN E. O'CONNOR

Flush with praise of *The Birth of a Nation* in 1916, D. W. Griffith predicted that within ten years all students would learn their history lessons by watching movies rather than by reading books. According to this logic, if films were made with due attention to historical accuracy, the students who watched them would be transported into the past, where they would meet historical figures face-to-face and witness events firsthand, rather than having to read static, secondhand descriptions. That Griffith's prediction was mistaken is evident from the millions of dollars still being made by textbook publishers. That his rationale was wrong as well is one of the central premises of this discussion. History teachers should be less concerned with having students try to re-experience the past and more concerned with teaching them how to learn from the study of it. Keeping this in mind, teachers should integrate more critical film and television analysis into their history classes, but not in place of reading and not at the expense of traditional approaches.

The moving-image media in which Griffith was pioneering in the early twentieth century have a tremendous impact on society and culture today. For history teachers, both the opportunities and the pressures are great. The days of quirky projectors and torn, brittle 16-mm prints are gone, swept away in the video revolution. Wonderful software resources are available: feature films on cassette, school licensing and off-air taping of television specials, videodisks that can be programmed for interactive learning, and much more. But the availability of the media materials must remain secondary to what the teacher tries to accomplish with them. Indeed, some teachers should perhaps use less film and video, but analyze what they do use more critically.

Griffith was impressed with the power of his camera to recreate the past; he wanted students to sit back and let themselves be carried away by his films. However, if the goal of education is to teach rather than entertain, teachers must, in contrast, show students how to engage, rather than suspend, their critical faculties when the projector or the TV monitor is turned on. This approach may require that the teacher take considerably more time to prepare for a film-oriented lesson, but when carefully integrated into the course, and when properly handled by the sensitive teacher, lessons based in film and television analysis can improve the effectiveness of history teaching. Although unmotivated by history per se, students may find themselves caught up in "doing" history before they realize what has happened to them.

In the 1970s and early 1980s, the academic field of history, like the humanities in general, underwent a series of challenges. Students who wanted skills they could use in the job market saw little reason to study what many perceived as an irrelevant past. At the same time, scholars turned to sophisticated statistical and other techniques and further specialized the subjects of their research. The gap between current historical scholarship and what was taught in the typical history classroom widened. Exciting as new investigative approaches may have been, it became more difficult for teachers in high schools and in introductory college survey courses to integrate the conclusions of current research into their everyday classes. For some, introductory-level history teaching became stale. Just as historians perceived a widening gulf between what interested them as researchers and what they had to teach in the classroom, so students—driven to worry more about training for an occupation—saw even less clearly the relevance of history courses to their future lives.

The most common applications of film and television in the history or social studies classroom today reflect that staleness. Films are often used for programmed learning (conveying a body of information that would be particularly difficult or time-consuming for teachers to develop on their own) or for sensitizing the class to a subject or giving the students the "feeling" of an era. The moving-image media serve these functions well, because they can present complex information and transport students across space and time so that distant events and far-flung parts of the world seem more real and relevant. Discussions based on the group experience of a class viewing a film may be more productive than discussions of homework reading assignments, and poor readers and otherwise hard-to-motivate students may find it easier to participate. Yet each such use, pragmatic as it may seem, may also serve to reinforce the passive pattern of viewing that students develop in front of their televisions at home. If teachers were to devote some of their efforts to a more active analytical approach to film and television, the moving-image media would better serve the history classroom.

Almost every course in the history curriculum lends itself to at least some dimension of relevant film or television analysis. In addition to helping communicate subtle aspects of historical subject matter, the structuring of a critical analysis of visual materials within the context of traditional historical methodology helps to teach students the basic elements of historical thinking, gives them firsthand experience in the process, and aids them in dealing more intelligently with the kinds of communications media they will face outside of school.

All historians and history educators, especially in the context of an open and democratic society, have a broader responsibility to the public and their students than simply relating the events of the past. They must also provide members of society with the skills of critical evaluation necessary to perform as responsible citizens. Thirty years ago, students had to be taught to read the newspaper critically, to identify bias, and to distinguish between factual reporting and editorializing. Today, when more people claim to get their news about the world from TV than from newspapers, students also need to learn skills of critical evaluation for the viewing of film and television. While most students are probably more familiar with TV than teachers would wish, few students understand the ways this medium affects (and often misleads) them. Students need to understand how the construction of the typical TV news interview is an expression of technological limitations and media conventions. Similarly, they should learn to be sensitive to the ways political television commercials may unconsciously appeal to their feelings and emotions rather than to their intellectual judgment.

When educators accept the responsibility of teaching students not to believe everything that appears in print, they endorse the American tradition of freedom of expression and give students the tools with which to survive in a free marketplace of ideas. Likewise, teachers must prepare their students to critically evaluate the audiovisual messages they receive. The freedom a democratic society allows to media producers implies a direct challenge to educators to teach students to interpret critically and evaluate everything that they see in the media. There is no more appropriate person for teaching these lessons than the history or social studies teacher, and no more appropriate place for such learning to take place than in the history classroom.

Another goal of history and social studies education is to encourage students to adopt habits of lifelong learning and to provide them with the analytical skills they will need in order to learn from their future experiences. The growing frequency of historically oriented television dramas and miniseries offers a challenge to teachers. It would be a mistake to presume that because of such programs the public is developing more of a historical consciousness than it had before. What can be assumed, however, is that whatever the average person today does know (or presumes to know) about history is much less likely to come from books than from film and TV. It might be argued that a steady diet of television docudramas and pseudo-docudramas, from "Plymouth Plantation" to "Roots" and "Watergate," from "I Claudius" to "Shogun" and "The Winds of War," has begun to undermine whatever respect there might have been in the public mind for the work of the professional historian and history teacher. Without having read a book or gone near a classroom, millions of viewers in 1981 thought that they had learned much about the American Civil War by watching several evenings of "The Blue and the Gray."

The ever-present implication of most popular productions is that history is no more than a straightforward story to be told like any other narrative. In such a simple context there is no room for subtle shadings of interpretation. In the stories that make for successful movies or television programs, the motives of major characters must be understandable in terms of present-day values and concerns immediately accessible to a general audience, and there must always be a satisfying conclusion. Network touting of the research that went into the design of sets and costumes (characteristically greater than that which went into a thoughtful presentation of genuinely important historical issues) encourages the public to understand a production as the most accurate portrayal possible. The study guides that many productions provide for teachers may suggest questions for classroom discussion or sources for additional information, but they never explain how the requirements of producing for popular television may have forced the simplification of complex historical characters and intricate patterns of causation to near caricature, nor do they acknowledge that there may be very different but equally defensible interpretations of the issues and events portrayed.

Scholars and teachers, people professionally committed to understanding and practicing the intellectual rigors of historical methodology and interpretation, must defend against the notion that history is no more than storytelling and the historian no more than a storyteller, stringing together dates and details and arbitrarily moving characters around as though they were actors on the set of "Eleanor and Franklin." Students should learn that there is no such thing as a completely objective or absolutely true historical account in print or on film, and should become sensitive to the often complex ways moving-image media invariably interpret what they present.

The need to analyze film in the history classroom should be measured against the relative importance of teaching students to evaluate critically what they encounter in textbooks or journal articles. Once they have finished with their high school or college courses, how many are likely to read a history textbook or subscribe to the *American Historical Review*? It may be myopic to spend so much precious class time dealing with the sources important to scholars and specialists, without taking at least a few hours each term to help develop the skills students will need to view more critically the historical documentaries and docudramas from which they will more likely learn their history in future years. Teachers should be less concerned with identifying factual mistakes on the screen and more with alerting students to the characteristic ways popular film and television productions often manipulate and trivialize historical issues. Students should be taught how to question the images they see on the screen, just as they are urged to look for loaded words or phrases in a book or newspaper. For example, they can be made aware of the potential for bias and misrepresentation in the creative use of music and sound effects and in the presentation of staged or studio-produced stock footage as though it were actuality footage (film of events, unstaged and unrehearsed, as they actually took place). Likewise, they should become alert for such techniques as an emotive sound track or improbable camera positions in footage presumed to be documentary. On the positive side, heightened awareness will enable students to understand the ways sensitive filmmakers can use their medium to address serious historical questions in unique ways.

How can film analysis be fit into an already crowded curriculum? Educators may need to re-think the goals of their teaching and remember that they must do more than simply fill students with information. Would a class period taken to discuss the elements of historical interpretation inherent in several clips from *The Return of Martin Guerre* distract a class from their textbook survey of early modern Europe? Would two or three class periods devoted to a close study of *The Plow That Broke the Plains* as a propaganda effort for Roosevelt's New Deal be off the track of a syllabus in American history? Would a ten-minute analysis of the famous "Daisy Spot" political commercial from the 1964 Lyndon Johnson presidential campaign be a digression for a class learning about the evolution of the electoral process in the twentieth century? These and other films, which will be used as examples in the following pages, are included among the thirteen selections in a two-hour video compilation intended to provide teachers with the materials necessary to begin to practice the approaches suggested in this discussion. The selections also include examples of newsreel footage and television news, a Nazi propaganda film, a recent historical documentary, a historical docudrama made for public television, and several often-cited examples from the early histories of both film and television. A printed guide to the compilation includes support materials for each selection, many of which can be photocopied for class distribution.

ANALYZING A MOVING IMAGE AS
A HISTORICAL DOCUMENT

One approach to the analysis of film and television programs parallels the way a written document is studied. The moving-image selection is treated as a historical document and studied using methods that reinforce historical thinking and develop students' skills of visual literacy. The term *moving-image document* refers to any form of the motion picture technology descended from that developed in the 1890s: from Edison's earliest experiments to last night's TV news; from classic documentaries to TV sitcoms; from factual footage such as the Zapruder film of the Kennedy assassination to the complete fantasy of some TV docudramas; from relatively "value-free" and undeniably accurate images such as the unedited filmed records of scientific experiments to the unbridled propaganda of Leni Riefenstahl and the only slightly more subtle manipulations of everyday television commercials. Calling these visual examples documents may seem strange at first, but the term allows teachers and students to approach moving images with the traditional tools of historical analysis.

There are two stages in the analysis of a moving-image document. Taken together, they provide a coherent and comprehensive methodology for historians when studying film and television and integrating moving-image media into the research and teaching of history. The first stage involves the general analysis of the document in order to establish as much information as possible about it. While certain data will be evident at first viewing, a more thorough analysis will require that students explore questions of the document's content, production, and reception through:

- A close study of the content of the film itself, that is, the images that appear on the screen, the sounds on the sound track, and the ways they are brought together to convey meaning;

- An investigation of the social, cultural, political, economic, and institutional background of the production and the conditions under which the film was made; and

- An examination of the ways the film or television program was understood by its original audiences.

In the second stage, the data or information gathered in the first stage is endowed with deeper meaning in relation to some type of historical inquiry. The many and varied ways in which scholars and teachers have made use of moving-image documents can be reduced to four frameworks for historical inquiry:

- Moving-image documents as representations of history;

- Moving-image documents as evidence for social and cultural history;

- Moving-image documents as evidence for historical fact; and

- Moving-image documents as evidence for the history of film and television.

In the first framework the moving image is studied as a secondary document, but the remaining three frameworks are contexts in which film and television can be used as primary sources. Although many moving-image documents might be analyzed using multiple frameworks, each calls different analytical concerns to the fore and assigns more or less significance to different aspects of the data collected in the first stage.

Stage One: General Analysis of a Moving-Image Document

Historians characteristically ask three types of questions of any document or artifact: questions about content, production, and reception. Generations of history teachers have successfully applied this technique when analyzing written documents with their classes. In a lesson on the 1776 Declaration of Independence, for example, the teacher would ask what the content of the document was, that is, what did the declaration itself say? Students then might break the document into its constituent parts: a preamble and a paragraph-long explication of the theory of popular sovereignty and the right of revolution, followed by a catalog of grievances held against the king and a closing proclamation of independence. Once the structure of the document was understood, students would consider the meaning and connotation of certain words, such as "unalienable" rights, and the likely derivation of pertinent phrases, such as "a long train of abuses" evincing a "design," which they would find had been drawn directly from Locke's *Second Treatise on Government*. Students would then discuss what might have been deliberately omitted from the document and the reasons for it, perhaps noting the absence of any reference to slavery.

Next, questions about the production of the document would center on the precedents for such public declarations, the makeup of the Second Continental Congress, the personalities and values of the people involved, the experience of previous efforts to deal with the British, the need to foster the support of the many colonists hesitant to make such a break, and the overriding fact that war had been under way since April 1775. Each of these factors and many more would have to be kept in mind if the students were to fully understand why this document took the shape that it did.

Finally, in terms of the reception of the document, the students would note the document's significance to people like George Washington and his soldiers, who until this point had fought as an army of rebellion in the name of a nation too timid to declare its intentions. The document also put pressure on uncommitted colonists to choose sides, and it helped American diplomats in Europe who were trying to arrange for foreign assistance in the war. Students might also consider the significance of the document in terms of later experience, such as its relevance to the abolition movement of the nineteenth century or Third World liberation movements in the twentieth century.

The searching inquiry of each of these factors makes the technique of documentary analysis valuable in the teaching of history. In addition to raising for discussion the complex nexus of related issues and events and introducing various theories of causation, such an approach provides students with valuable experience in carefully analyzing meaning, identifying bias, and evaluating significance with regard to written or published documents, essential skills for any educated person.

Teachers can productively apply the same questions of content, production, and reception to the study of film and television documents:

- **Questions about content.** What information can be gleaned from the document itself, from a close study of what appears on the screen, through either direct or indirect analysis? What is included in the film? What is left out of it? How is this information determined by the visual and aural texture of the film? What is the connection between the medium and the message?

- **Questions about production.** What influences were at work in shaping the moving image document and, perhaps, served to limit or bias the information it conveys? Beyond the images themselves, how might the background (personal, political, professional) of the producer, director, actors, and others have influenced their performances? How might the institutional conventions and the larger purpose of the sponsoring agency (a Hollywood studio, an industrial organization, a Washington lobbying group) have colored the message of the production?

- **Questions about reception.** Regardless of the nuances of meaning that can be derived from an analysis of the film or TV production today (comparing it with other contemporaneous materials or judging it in the knowledge of what subsequently took place), what effect, if any, did it have on the pace or direction of events at the time it was made? Who saw the production and how might it have influenced them?

When these questions are applied to moving-image documents, classroom viewing is transformed from a passive to an active experience.

In the process, teachers engender in their students a healthy analytical skepticism, the first step toward informed comprehension.

There are different levels at which one can approach a Stage One analysis with a class. In terms of content, the second part of this discussion ("Visual Language") includes an explanation of the cutaway simple enough to be used with any high school class. The strategy for content analysis will vary with the interest of the teacher, the age and ability of the students, and the overall goals of the course. Regardless of the level of analysis attempted, any such process would help develop historical judgment and improve visual literacy skills.

In terms of production, students and teachers at every level should be sensitive to the biases built into any document they bring to class. College majors or graduate students in American history might find it appropriate to take a course in the communications department on the history of the film industry. In contrast, even fourth- or fifth-graders watching an environmental film produced by their local utility company should be asked to consider how the filmmakers may have influenced (subtly or otherwise) what is presented. In the same way that knowing the context of the political debates of the 1770s offers insight into the meaning of the Declaration of Independence, awareness of the commercial and political pressures at work on filmmakers in Hollywood and elsewhere, and the dramatic conventions current in the moving-image industry at one time or another, cannot help but deepen the understanding of a moving-image document.

Challenging a class to consider the reception of a film such as *The Plow That Broke the Plains* (1936) or Edward R. Murrow's 1954 "See It Now: Report on Senator McCarthy," can be as instructive about the social and political complexion of the 1930s or 1950s as understanding reception of the Declaration of Independence would be about the revolutionary generation. It is appropriate for students to realize, on levels commensurate with their interests and abilities, that although scholars may have failed as yet to trace the precise avenues of the social and psychological influences of film and television, there is indeed an association between media messages and the societies that perceive them.

It may also be important to sensitize students to the concern for authentication and completeness as it applies to the moving-image document. With a manuscript document, scholars would be concerned first with dating and authenticating a new discovery, studying the age of the parchment or paper, making sure that the document was all in the same handwriting, and comparing the script with others known to be written by the supposed author. They would check that the document was complete, that no pages were missing or damaged, and that there were no internal references to people who lived or events that took place at a later date and no anachronistic language relative to the time proposed for the piece. Such concerns are more typically those of the research historian than the history teacher, and the teacher who brings a printed copy of the Declaration of Independence into the classroom rightly presumes that preliminary concerns have been dealt with—that the document has been dated, authenticated, checked for completeness, and carefully transcribed.

When factors of age or wear-and-tear result in pages of a written manuscript being missing, it is usually evident to the scholar. In film and television, however, missing material is more of a problem. Many, if not most, of the films in rental circulation today are missing footage, often destroyed by projectors or cannibalized by collectors. Unless a splice was made poorly, viewers are usually unaware that anything is missing. Students should also be aware that there may be different releases of a film, just as there are different editions of a book. Many schools that screen the Nazi propaganda classic *Triumph of the Will* (1935) show it in a forty-two-minute version, rather than taking the class time for the original two-hour film. While it would be interesting to study in detail the ways the shortened version differs from the longer original, students should at least be aware that there is a difference. Minor changes can be important too. For example, Alain Resnais, maker of the documentary *Night and Fog* (1955) on the horrors of the Nazi concentration camps, responded to pressure that he remove a shot from the film that showed a French officer cooperating with German troops. Once students have discussed matters of authentication and completeness, they will be ready to ask questions about content, production, and reception.

Questions about content. Focusing on the content of a moving-image document can be more difficult than analyzing a written one. This is due in part to the breadth of individual interpretation that the viewer brings to the watching experience. The ordinary analytical tools a teacher would use may prove inadequate when applied to moving images. To comprehend more than the surface content of a moving-image document, therefore, teachers must develop at least a basic knowledge of visual language, including the elements of a shot (duration, lighting, color, field size, composition, camera angle, camera movement, focus, lens characteristics, film stock, projection speed) and the editing techniques (fade, dissolve, wipe, cut) with which filmmakers communicate their ideas. (See the section on "Visual Language.") It would be foolish indeed to try to study the "Declaration of the Rights of Man and the Citizen" in the original text with students who cannot read French, yet teachers regularly show moving-image documents without addressing the language of images. The viewing process is complicated because, unlike the frustrated readers who do not know French, passive viewers unconsciously assume that they have fully comprehended the visual document. Untrained viewers may have taken in the message that the filmmakers meant them to (or manipulated them to), but this is never enough. Realizing that surface comprehension represents only the most rudimentary level of meaning, teachers would never be completely satisfied with that level of analysis when examining a written document. They must therefore learn to demand the same depth of analysis in regard to moving images.

Early filmmakers realized that film allowed them the ability to play with time and space. Edwin S. Porter, D. W. Griffith, and others pioneered in the use of editing to collapse and expand time (drawing out a chase for dramatic effect, for example), and to cut from one location to another as an enhancement to dramatic tension (as in intercutting between chaser and chased). Editing could transform an ordinary series of images into an extraordinary one. An interesting historical example is the famous footage of Hitler's jig after stepping from the railway car in which he had accepted the surrender of France in 1940. This event never took place. With the help of a laboratory device called an optical printer, a team of patriotic British film editors was able to take an otherwise benign image of Hitler raising his leg and turn it into a diabolical dance. Shown on the newsreel screens of all the Allied nations at a psychological low point in the struggle against Nazism, the footage became powerful propaganda, a force for re-dedicating opposition against the heartless Führer. Filmmakers do not necessarily set out to misrepresent, but the creative tools they use nevertheless reshape and manipulate reality. Because questions of time, place, and reality are of concern to researchers and teachers of history, they must become fluent in the rhetoric of images.

The first step is to look closely at the image. For a moving image, close viewing requires repeated viewing, as well as an awareness of the technical tools developed by specialists in cinema studies and the ability to apply them where appropriate. One reason for using a short film with a class, even a single TV news story or a commercial, is that it can be shown several times. Another approach is to show a longer film once, and then repeat one segment of it several times for closer analysis. The video compilation designed to accompany this book includes a number of short films and selections from longer films and television productions chosen especially for the history classroom. One of the selections from this video compilation, *The Plow That Broke the Plains*, will be used to illustrate moving-image analysis.

The analytical process should involve the conscious segmenting of the document, parsing it as one would a sentence, to perceive patterns in its structure and form that also communicate meaning, but which might not be apparent at first viewing. *The Plow That Broke the Plains*, a twenty-eight-minute documentary film made by the United States government in 1936, is composed of seven major sequences:

- "Prologue," which identifies the Great Plains area and its environmental history as the subject for the film;

- "Settlement," which details the arrival of the ranchers and farmers;

- "Warning," which recounts the impact of one of the cyclical droughts in the area that should have led settlers and policymakers to act differently;

- "Wheat Will Win the War," which explains the influence of World War I on the rapid agricultural development of the plains area;

- "Twenties Boom," which shows the mechanization of farms and the speculation that led to continuing overdevelopment in the 1920s;

- "Dust Bowl," which details the overwhelming impact of the mid-1930s drought and the resulting dust storms; and

- "Migration," which shows how farmers were forced to abandon their homesteads and travel west to California looking for work.

To understand how the structuring, ordering, and connecting of these sequences contributed to the information and point of view presented by the film, the class must outline these segments and analyze them in some detail. But even more information is needed if the class is to understand the controversy that surrounded the release of *The Plow* in the 1930s, when accusations of propaganda were raised against it. The first release of the film in April 1936 included a three-minute epilogue that explicitly credited the programs of the Roosevelt administration with responding to the plight of the people uprooted by the plains disaster. This epilogue, which contained the film's most forthright propaganda message, was removed as early as four weeks after the original release. The shorter ending to the film was a simple fade out from an image of a dead tree with an abandoned bird's nest (Figure A). The video compilation includes both endings so that students can compare and contrast.

A moving-image document usually communicates through visual signs and symbols and through the mixing of these visual elements with the dialogue and music on the sound track. In "Settlement," there is an image of a sledgehammer striking the top of a wooden stake; in "Warning," a small child is pictured sprawled on the dusty ground near an abandoned plow (Figure B); in a montage in "Twenties Boom," belching smokestacks are intercut with several shots of a ticker-tape machine that speeds up, teeters on its platform, and eventually crashes to the floor (Figure C). Each of these images derives its symbolic meaning in slightly different ways. The shot of the sledgehammer on the wooden stake is based on a cultural code, the tradition on the American frontier

Figure A

Figure B

Figure C

Figure D

of "staking" a claim to a piece of land. This meaning might be read independently, but it is reinforced by the context of the shot in a sequence dealing with the settlement of the frontier. The series of shots of the telegraphic ticker that eventually falls to the floor is arranged so that it almost has to refer to the 1929 "crash" of the stock market. The belching smokestacks, on the other hand, rely for their meaning almost completely on their visual context. Though the very same images in a different film might be intended to signify the bleakness and dirtiness of industrial life, in *The Plow* they represent surging productivity.

The image of the child and the plow is open to widely divergent interpretive readings, and students should be encouraged to work out the alternatives. One view, for example, is that the drought and the dust storms made the farmers and their tools as ineffective as a child in coping with the environment. A slightly different view suggests that the people who farmed the land were as innocent as "babes" in the face of great environmental forces (a view that seems to be at odds with the overall message of the film, which records how ambitious farmers overdeveloped and overcultivated the land, leaving insufficient grass cover to hold the moisture in dry years).

There are also interesting ways editing is used to create content in *The Plow*, although they are almost always open to interpretation. In "Wheat Will Win the War," images of farm tractors are intercut with pictures of tanks in battle. On one level, this is a visual way to dramatize the contributions of farmers to the war effort, but others might interpret these scenes as a comment on the impact new farm technology had on the delicate ecology of the plains. Some viewers might understand the cut from the "crash" of the ticker-tape machine to a bleached skull lying on the parched earth (Figure D) as a simple chronological transition from the 1920s to the 1930s; others might read ideological meaning into that juxtaposition, suggesting that financial collapse and environmental disaster may somehow have been connected, perhaps by causes rooted in the capitalist system.

A detailed effort to comprehend the signs and symbols present in a film is essential to a thorough analysis of its content. The meaning of images may seem self-evident, but it almost always depends on an interaction or negotiation between the viewer and the moving image being viewed. The only time that it is correct to think of film as a static object is when it is rolled up in its can on the shelf. Any effort to elucidate meaning from a moving image demands a consideration of the spectator. For the historian, this often means a spectator from some past time.

Another element of content that must be considered is the sound track. The sound track of a film or television document can, at times, be more important than the visual information, and the sound track always influences the way the images are understood. When watching silent films, it is important to remember that they would have almost always been shown with musical accompaniment—an orchestra, a piano, or even a phonograph. Dialogue, narration, sound effects, and music all contribute to the message content of a moving-image document. For example, the authoritative voice of the narrator in *The Plow* is an important aural reinforcement of the film's claim to truth. The musical score for the film, by composer Virgil Thomson, adds additional impact. Based in part on quotations from traditional Amercan folk music, Thomson's "Suite for *The Plow That Broke the Plains*" has for years been available as an audio recording independent from the film, and is worth study as a piece of evocative music as well as the accompaniment to the film.

To summarize, although study of content (defined here as the information that can be gleaned from the close study of the images themselves on the screen) is the approach a historian would normally take to any document, a moving-image document may require resorting to different kinds of tools. Teachers who turn to film as evidence must give serious consideration to the nature of visual communication. They must familiarize themselves with at least some of the technical terminology used to characterize the elements of a motion-picture shot and the types of editing devices available to the filmmaker. The insights of scholars who bring linguistic, psychological, and other theoretical constructs to the study of cinema and television should also be considered. To the extent that anyone who sits down to study a film has at least an unconscious assumption about what a film is and how it communicates its message, each person brings some concept of theory to the task of analysis.

Questions about production. Whereas content analysis deals with what is on the screen, production analysis probes the background elements, how and why things made it to the screen. When studying a letter or a diary entry as a piece of evidence, historians seek to put themselves in the place of the author, trying to understand the conditions under which the document was written and how those conditions may have influenced its content. To some extent, therefore, the analysis of a moving-image document requires learning something about how and why it was produced.

Manuscripts or printed documents are often the product of one person, but such individual authorship is rare in moving-image documents. Despite the tendency of some critics to credit one auteur with the style and presentation of a production, most film and television scholars now recognize that productions are the result of complex collaborative efforts in which scores of people (including producers, directors, screenwriters, cinematographers, editors, actors, and publicists) contribute creative ideas at various stages in the process. To some extent, understanding of this collaborative process has been demonstrated most clearly by historians who have combed studio and other archives in search of a "paper trail" to document the moving-image production process.

The production background of *The Plow* offers some interesting illustrations.[1] This film was, more than most, the work of an individual artist. Pare Lorentz had been a film critic and an outspoken booster of the Roosevelt administration before he won the approval of the Resettlement Administration, one of the myriad new "alphabet" agencies set up in the early days of the New Deal, to make his first film. The Resettlement Administration wanted a movie that could be used to train its many new employees and introduce them to the agency's goals, which were to provide rehabilitation loans to farm families and to facilitate the resettlement of people from depressed areas of the country to places where there were better opportunities for employment. The Great Plains, a depressed area that was suffering from environmental as well as economic woes, held special interest for Lorentz. In addition, the Resettlement Administration was impressed by Lorentz's insistence that such a film could be made with production values advanced enough to allow commercial release as well. The agency had drawn sharp criticism from those opposed to Roosevelt's policies, because it represented the increasing role of government in social planning, and it saw the film as a much desired opportunity to explain and defend its programs. Moreover, Lorentz wanted to utilize the dramatic power of the medium to convince audiences to accept his film's important social and political messages.

Lorentz's decision to produce and direct the film himself was the first of many driven by the spartan $6,000 budget authorized for the project. It was immediately decided that he would not hire actors, rent studio facilities, or attempt to record sound on location. On-screen animations would be kept simple and inexpensive (as indeed is the opening map animation in the film). Lorentz refused to compromise on the quality of his technical crew, however. As camera operators he chose Ralph Steiner, Paul Strand, and Leo Hurwitz, all experienced and talented filmmakers in their own right. Each had already established a personal vision in his own work and would go on to a long and important career. As the team proceeded through a seven-week tour of filming locations in Montana, Wyoming, Colorado, Kansas, and Texas, however, it became clear that their vision was not the same as that of Lorentz. Steiner and Hurwitz, who would later found their own radical leftist group under the name Frontier Films, complained that Lorentz did not have a clear enough plan for the film he was making and that he failed to see the economic roots of the problems he wanted to explain. Lorentz remembered that "they wanted it to be all about human greed and how lousy our social

---

[1] For more details on the background of Pare Lorentz and *The Plow*, see the guide to the video compilation and Robert L. Snyder, *Pare Lorentz and the Documentary Film* (Norman, Okla., 1968).

16

system was."[2] As a Roosevelt loyalist, Lorentz was not prepared to go this far. He rejected the alternative script the two proposed and, after shooting enough dust-storm footage, he released the crew.

The remaining footage necessary for the film was to be stock footage purchased from newsreel companies and Hollywood studios, but the leaders of the movie capital proved uncooperative. The movie industry people feared government involvement in movie production and did all they could to make access difficult.[3] Lorentz had to rely on the personal assistance of his friend King Vidor to get the needed footage from the studio libraries: footage of giant mule-driven combines at work on the plains, of World War I battle scenes, and of parades of returning troops, among others. Before returning from California, Lorentz shot the closing scenes of the roadside migrant camp, with the assistance of still photographer Dorothea Lange, who personally lined up cars along the road.[4]

Back in New York, having spent far more than his original budget (the final cost would come to just under $20,000), Lorentz still had to edit his film and have a musical score written for it. Not knowing how much money he could promise as a fee, the novice filmmaker convinced a bright young composer who had never written a film score to work with him. The collaboration between Pare Lorentz and Virgil Thomson was uniquely creative because of the way that they worked together. Typically, the editing of a film is finished first and the narration recorded; then the composer is called in to write music to fit it. Lorentz took a different approach in *The Plow* (and in his second film, *The River* [1937]), which resulted in an interesting interplay between the images and the musical score. First, he and Thomson discussed at length the kinds of traditional and folk music that should be quoted in various sequences. Lorentz provided the composer with a rough cut of the film to guide his work to timed sequences, and once the music was written, Lorentz projected each sequence of the film as Thomson played his score on the piano. Once approved, the score was orchestrated and recorded. In a significant departure from standard practice, Lorentz then took the recorded score back to the editing room and re-edited the film, adjusting the sequence and timing of the images where necessary to fit the music or, at times, to use the music as a counterpoint for the visual presentation.[5] The end result was a unique marriage of music and film (which was even more impressive in *The River*).

By understanding the process of the production of this film, viewers can comprehend it much more fully. By explaining that the problems of the dust bowl were largely due to unplanned and overambitious agricultural development, first by ranchers, then by small independent farmers,

[2] Snyder, *Pare Lorentz*, 31.
[3] Richard Dyer MacCann, *The People's Films* (New York, 1973), 68.
[4] Snyder, *Pare Lorentz*, 31-32.
[5] Ibid., 33-37.

and finally by mechanized farms and corporate land companies in the wake of war-driven increased demand for grain, the film rationalized the need for agencies such as the Resettlement Administration to bring conservation, planning, and organized redevelopment to the area. Viewers aware of the arguments that Lorentz had with his politically radical film crew should better understand the relatively moderate ideological point of view that the film assumed. More specifically, they may be less disappointed by the rather rudimentary style of the map animation at the beginning of the film, possible mistakes in continuity, and transitions that confuse historical issues, once aware of the financial and creative restrictions under which the filmmaker worked. Finally, students may be more appreciative of the interplay of image, narration, and music when they know something about Lorentz's feeling for all three and his unique procedures for bringing them together.

The social and political influences at work in the production process may be more or less explicit, but they must be taken into account for a complete analysis of any document. Hollywood entertainment films offer numerous examples. Jack Warner's support for FDR and involvement in the writing of the National Recovery Administration code for the motion-picture industry clearly influenced the pro-New Deal films made by Warner Brothers in the early 1930s. To view these films without this knowledge limits the insights that can be drawn from them. Any attempt at analysis of a social-problem film like *Wild Boys of the Road* (1934), without a realization that the form had become a genre in its own right, would surely invite a misreading. Every film or television program has a production history that helps to explain it as a document. While there is not as much known about the production of most films as about that of *The Plow*, historians and film scholars have amassed a great deal of background information about many important moving-image documents. Teachers should choose carefully the films they bring to class (as the selections in the video compilation have been chosen), with an eye to the background information that is available to support classroom analysis. No matter what film is used in class, students should be asked to consider, at least in a hypothetical way, the reasons for the making of the film and the forces that may have been at work in its production.

Questions about reception. Questions about reception have been most troublesome for film scholars and historians alike. Many assertions have been made regarding the direct impact of film and television on society. The *Payne Fund Studies* of the 1930s associated movie watching with juvenile delinquency and a perceived decline of morals in the United States. More recently, television viewing has been used as a defense in the courtroom, with a defendant's attorney claiming that the client had been brainwashed by the violence on TV and left unable to distinguish right from wrong. Neither of these efforts offered convincing proof of the negative effects of the moving-image media on viewers.

How can the impact of a film or television program on its audience be evaluated? Published reviews are available, but each represents only one individual's point of view. Studio commercial records, where available, and trade newspapers such as *Variety* provide some data on the financial success of many productions, but there is no certain way to measure the impact of even the most popular production on the people who saw it.

Much of the current work in cinema studies involves what is termed reception analysis. If a film communicates its message through visual symbols that derive their meaning at least in part from the viewer's individual personality, cultural values, or experience with other films, then the viewer must be involved in the construction of that meaning. An older "illusionist" position argues that films create the illusion of reality, which spectators simply absorb as passive receptacles. Today this older view has been replaced by a much more complex understanding of reception in which the viewer is an active agent in the making of meaning from a film. In analyzing the *Classical Hollywood Cinema* (New York, 1985), David Bordwell borrows from art historian E. M. Gombrich in suggesting that filmmakers build upon traditional formal patterns for the ways of presenting things, "schemata," as he calls them, which have been normalized over years of studio production. After looking at scores of films, viewers have become experienced at interpreting these schemata and have developed a series of "mental sets" through which they process the images presented to them. The viewing of a film, then, is not a passive experience; rather, the audience tests each twist in the plot, each cinematic event, against the relevant mental set. If subsequent shots do not obey the schemata, viewers turn to the next most likely alternative. Piecing together the meaning of a film thus represents a complex negotiation between filmmakers and viewers.[6]

Another problem relates to the varying experiences and frames of mind that any audience brings to a moving-image experience. Different cultural experiences, different racial or class associations, and different sexual or political predispositions all influence the ways people carry on this negotiation. To some extent, therefore, every viewer, or at least every group of viewers distinguished by differences of class, race, or gender, sees their own film. Feminist film criticism, for example, concentrates on studying how films make meaning for women.

When teachers watch *The Plow* with their students today, they see it differently than audiences did in 1936. This is due in part to the far broader experience today's audiences have had with visual communications. The compositional style (comparable to documentary pho-

[6] David Bordwell, Janet Staiger, and Kristin Thompson, *The Classical Hollywood Cinema: Film Style and Mode of Production to 1960* (New York, 1985), 7-9.

tographs of the period), the black-and-white (rather than color) images, and the pattern and pace of some of the editing may strike today's viewers as dull in comparison to the dynamic, colorful, and almost frenetically paced images of television. More important in understanding this film as a historical document, however, is recognizing that the values, concerns, and experiences of the people of the 1930s influenced the way those viewers saw the film. Even then, it would have had different meanings for different audiences. *The Plow* would have met with varying receptions in New York or Oklahoma, among businesspeople, farmers threatened with eviction, or displaced migrants. To some extent, today's viewers may also be influenced by subsequent films they have seen about life in thirties America such as *The Grapes of Wrath* (1940) or TV series such as "The Waltons."

Most critics of the 1930s were generous in their praise of *The Plow That Broke the Plains.* A few thought it was too dreary or depressing, but others noted the importance of getting this message to the American public. Still, Lorentz found only limited success in his attempts to have the film screened commercially. There were a few presentations in first-run theaters in New York, Chicago, and other cities, but the film was refused by the large booking circuits that dictated the programs for the nation's major theater chains. Lorentz and the staff of the Resettlement Administration went to work in the Midwest during the summer of 1936 trying to book the film in independent theater chains, and they had some success. In the end, due to direct promotion, there were as many as 3,000 commercial theaters that showed the film. This was not a bad showing, considering the total of approximately 14,000 commercial theaters operating in the country in 1936, but it was not what Lorentz had hoped for.[7]

One presentation of which the filmmaker was particularly proud was under the auspices of the Museum of Modern Art, in which *The Plow* was screened on the same bill with government-sponsored films of other nations, such as Germany's *Triumph of the Will.*[8] In this context, there was no mistaking Lorentz's intention to have his film present a propagandistic message.

President Roosevelt was ecstatic after seeing the film in a special White House screening. *Time* magazine reported that Roosevelt had actually considered sending the film to Congress in place of a presidential message.[9] But FDR's congressional critics, still a minority but riding high on court decisions that were supporting their efforts to deflate the New Deal and tear down its hierarchy of new social agencies, were particularly inflamed. They noted that 1936 was a presidential

[7] Snyder, *Pare Lorentz*, 47.

[8] See Lorentz's letter to Stephen J. Early at the White House, 12 May 1936, in the guide to the video compilation.

[9] *Time*, 25 May 1936, quoted in MacCann, *People's Films*, 78-79.

election year, and that by actively promoting public screenings of *The Plow*, the agency was spreading propaganda for the administration (and, by definition, against the Republicans). The most avid criticism of the film came from those who objected to the broad brush used by the film to identify the blighted region. A regional administrator from Texas complained to Resettlement Administration chief Rexford Guy Tugwell that the film's generalizations about the areas devastated by soil erosion and dust storms made *The Plow* unusable in his part of the country. A Democratic Texas state representative called the film "a libel on the greatest section of the United States" and threatened to punch Tugwell in the nose if he did not have the film destroyed.[10]

The deleting of the epilogue from the film may have helped to blunt the charges of propaganda, but it did nothing to soften the political opposition or the protest from the plains region. Eventually, the combination of Republican opposition and regional criticism led to the film's withdrawal from circulation in 1940. It remained on the shelf until the early 1960s.

The controversy over *The Plow* affected subsequent government film projects. Since World War II, the American government has spent hundreds of millions of dollars making films about every aspect of American life and society for use in informational and educational programs overseas. Concern over potential domestic charges of political propaganda, which was bred in part by the controversy over *The Plow That Broke the Plains*, led Congress to forbid the screening of all but a few of these films in the United States.

The reception experience with television is very different from that with the big screen. Whatever illusion of reality there may be in the darkened theater is broken, or at least altered, in the context of the living room. The viewing experience must be understood in the context of the flow of programming, for example, from a news broadcast to a quiz show to a baseball game, all punctuated by commercial interruptions. Watching TV with other people is characterized by very different patterns of personal courtesy; people are much more willing to carry on a conversation over a TV program in their living room (or to tolerate one going on around them) than they would be in a movie theater. Although people may not watch the TV screen as attentively as they do the movie screen, they watch TV more frequently, and therefore the repetition of TV messages, whether the generalized messages of violence in police dramas or the repetition of specific commercial messages, may have more cumulative impact. Finally, because for many people the same electronic box serves both as their prime source for news information and as their major source of everyday entertainment, television necessarily influences the ways people make meaning about the world around them.

[10] See the guide to the video compilation.

There are cases in which the reception of a moving-image document has been linked to the progress of historical events. The history of television and recent American politics offers such interesting examples as the impact of Walter Cronkite's February 1968 special report from Vietnam on Lyndon Johnson's decision not to run for a second complete term, and the role of Roger Mudd's special interview with Edward Kennedy in defeating his bid for the 1980 presidential nomination. Edward R. Murrow's 1954 "See It Now: Report on Senator McCarthy" has often been credited with beginning to turn the public mind against the senator, although there had already been many print and at least a few radio journalists who had taken that stand. Certainly the credibility that Murrow had with the American public must be considered a factor in the reception of the broadcast, and the tens of thousands of letters and telegrams CBS received (90 percent of them agreeing with the program) cannot be discounted. But absolute proof is elusive. The televised Army McCarthy hearings that began only a few weeks later have also been credited with deflating McCarthy, but it has elsewhere been pointed out that only a few stations carried those hearings in full. Whenever thoughtful scholars have addressed the problem of audience impact, they have noted the complexity of the connection.[11] Although it is difficult to make precise connections, a growing amount of literature discusses the intersection of media reception and culture. Most impressive is the National Institute of Mental Health's summary of research on the impact of television on American society, *Television and Behavior: Ten Years of Scientific Progress and Implications for the Eighties*, Vol. 1, *Summary Report* (Washington, D.C., 1983), which makes categorical statements on subjects such as the relation of TV violence and attitudes among youth.[12]

Popular writers have been quicker to suggest how changes in social values can be credited to popular films. Style in the wearing (or not wearing) of men's undershirts, for example, has been traced to the barechested appearance of Clark Gable in *It Happened One Night* (1932). More important examples center on the changing roles of women and racial minorities, but these speculations are still impressionistic and substantially undocumented. Direct correlation is often difficult to prove because the patterns of reflection and refraction that form the connection between screen images and social values are so complex.

[11] See, for example, Gregory W. Bush, "Edward Kennedy and the Televised Personality in the 1980 Presidential Campaign," and Daniel Leab, *"See It Now: A Legend Reassessed,"* in John E. O'Connor, ed., *American History/American Television: Interpreting the Video Past* (New York, 1983), 1-32.; David Culbert has written on LBJ and the Cronkite broadcast in "Johnson and the Media," in Robert A. Divine, ed., *Exploring the Johnson Years* (Austin, Texas, 1981), 214-48.
[12] See also Joshua Meyrowitz, *No Sense of Place: The Impact of Electronic Media on Social Behavior* (New York, 1985).

Stage Two: Four Frameworks for Historical Inquiry

Once the basic questions about the content, production, and reception of a moving-image document have been asked and answered as fully as possible, there are a number of ways the history scholar or teacher can proceed. Just as a diplomatic historian and a psycho-biographer might look very differently at the same document, for example, Henry Kissinger's personal diary, so there are various frameworks for analysis that can be applied to a moving-image document. The four frameworks for historical inquiry include: moving-image documents as representations of history; moving-image documents as evidence for social and cultural history; moving-image documents as evidence for historical fact; and moving-image documents as evidence for the history of film and television.

The value of any document depends on the information one seeks to draw from it. No sensible research historian or history teacher would try to study the history of World War II using clips from newsreels as the major source of information. On almost any broad topic there are better sources in print. For more closely framed questions, however, such as the public's perception of the war as it proceeded, the newsreels, as well as the newspapers and magazines, of the period would be an important source. Though it may be best to withhold judgment on questions of cause and effect, Hollywood entertainment films and their counterparts in other cultures can serve as primary documents for the study of social and cultural history.

Films that portray history raise deeper issues. A film like *The Birth of a Nation*, despite its concentration on the institution of slavery and the experience of the Civil War and Reconstruction, is almost useless for studying those issues and events. Griffith was proud of his efforts to recreate precisely the interior of Ford's Theater and other sites, but his interpretation of the issues and events involved was based on his own prejudiced reading of the then-current secondary literature. Yet, in the proper frame of reference, viewing and analyzing *The Birth of a Nation* and studying the record of the public protests that accompanied its screening around the country, can be a rewarding experience in the history classroom.[13] This film is a particularly rich document for illustrating to students how the popular perception of historical subjects changes over time, as well as for studying the history of the developing industry and art form of the cinema.

In each of the four frameworks for historical inquiry, the different types of information sought from the documents dictate different analytical concerns, and different aspects of the content, production, and reception will therefore assume more or less importance. The four frameworks for historical inquiry are not meant to be rigid or limiting in any

---

[13] See Fred Silva, ed., *Focus on Birth of a Nation* (Englewood Cliffs, N.J., 1971).

way, nor should they suggest that a complex and dynamic field can be so neatly divided. In practice, there will always be an overlap among the four; no single framework can or should be applied without some reference to the others. Each serves to concentrate attention on the types of analytical issues about which teachers should be aware and to identify particular methodological concerns that may relate more to one framework than to another.

The four frameworks do not address different types of films, but different types of historical investigation. Any film is open to study under more than one of the frameworks. Newsreel footage of a protest demonstration, such as the 1932 Bonus Marchers recorded by Universal Newsreel (see the video compilation), might invite study in terms of all four frameworks. If the producers of the newsreel placed the event in the context of previous protest activity, the newsreel could be studied as an interpretation of recent history (Framework One). In a study of the social and cultural values inherent in the newsreel story (Framework Two), special attention would be devoted to the attitudes suggested in the editing of the images and in the words and tone of voice chosen for the narration. A scholar more concerned with the details of the event as it actually took place (Framework Three) would hope to transcend both the editors' and the narrator's points of view and use outtakes to try to reconstruct the raw, unedited footage of the event as it was originally shot. Finally, a historian of the movie industry (Framework Four) might find special meaning in the other stories included in the same newsreel, in the order and style in which the stories were presented, in the ways the newsreel company promoted its product, and in the cities and neighborhoods where theaters showed that company's newsreels rather than another's.

In the outline of the four frameworks for historical inquiry that follows, attention is directed to the ways in which the context of each framework heightens or diminishes the relative importance of content, production, and reception.

Framework One: Moving-image documents as representations of history. Perhaps the most obvious way the moving image relates to history is in the portrayal of historical events. By 1923, when the *Chronicles of America* series of films for the classroom was launched under the auspices of Yale University, commercial producers were already touting their skills at recreating the past. "It's history written in lightning,"[14] Woodrow Wilson was said to have responded to a White House screening of *The Birth of a Nation.*

[14] Thomas R. Cripps, "The Reaction of the Negro to the Motion Picture, *Birth of a Nation,*" *Historian,* 26 (1963): 344-62, reprinted in Silva, *Focus on The Birth of a Nation,* 115.

There is no such thing as a totally objective or absolutely true representation of the past, and it is foolish to think that anyone can experience the past through a filmed attempt to recreate it. Any film that deals with a historical subject interprets that subject in some way. The approach may be unintended or carefully designed; it may be explicit in the narration or implied in the visual context. Whether the film is a documentary or a Hollywood dramatization with costumed actors repeating scripted lines, every moving image, like every piece of writing, has a point of view. The challenge in understanding and fully appreciating moving-image documents as representations of history is to comprehend that point of view and the ways the visual and aural elements of the film contribute to its presentation.

It might seem at first glance that the documentary film made completely with archival actuality footage from the period in question would be by definition more accurate than a dramatization, but every choice of image, every joining of one image to another, and every word of narration or note of music added to the sound track represents a creative choice equivalent to the writer's composition of sentences and the combining of paragraphs and chapters into a book. Makers of dramatized films may have an even greater opportunity than documentarists to develop accurate historical situations because the mise-en-scène is so much more in their control.

There are several selections in the video compilation that lend themselves to this type of analysis with students. In some ways the most interesting example is a selection from *The Return of Martin Guerre* (1983), a film that uses a tale of marital abandonment and imposture to present a view of peasant life in sixteenth-century France. Natalie Zemon Davis, who served as historical consultant for the production of the film, was pleased with many aspects of the finished product and disappointed with others. Great effort was spent in creating the mise-en-scène as accurately as possible. Costumes, settings, language, and music were studied and designed with great care. Careful attention was also given to the interpretation of the events portrayed in the film—Davis was researching a book on the subject at the same time—but here she was less successful. The pressure to make a film that would appeal to general audiences led the producers to develop characters that would seem more real to twentieth-century viewers and to cast the story in the form of a whodunit, rather than as history. With regard to the characters, Davis argued for the pastness of the past, that is, the importance of recognizing that there were significant differences in the ways people thought and acted four hundred years ago. With regard to the story line, she suggested that a different narrative structure might have made the film a better vehicle for history, by privileging viewers in a different way and having them consider different issues and different points of view as the story progressed.

The visual texture of *The Return of Martin Guerre* is so rich and the story so engaging that any European history class would benefit from seeing it, but a closer analysis is needed to coax from the film the more subtle references to historical issues, such as the roles of marriage, law, property, and interpersonal relationships in the lives of sixteenth-century French peasants. A segmenting of the film into its major sequences, for example, would help to point up the treatment of these issues and would also make evident the ways the story had been structured to provoke maximum suspense and surprise in the audience. This structure may have optimized the entertainment value for a 1980s audience, but alternative structures may have offered better opportunity to develop key historical issues. For example, a narrative structure that allowed a more complex characterization of the central female character, Bertrande, would surely have addressed more of the women's history issues raised by her situation. Such questions of representation involve students in exciting discussions of the nature and meaning of history.

The video compilation also includes a segment from "Molders of Troy" (1983), a docudrama produced by historian Daniel Walkowitz for public television. There have now been several high-quality costume docudramas, and a score or more of compilation documentaries, that have involved professional historians from the outset, not merely as advisors but as full-fledged partners in positions of influence and control. This is certainly an encouraging development, but it should lead to no sense of security about future moving-image portrayals of the past. Because of his concern for the nature of history, historian-filmmaker Walkowitz explained that, as a scholar, he comes to a film project from a very different angle than the commercial producer. "I am less concerned with the authenticity of the details in a scene—for example, whether the shoes are authentic—than with the pattern of a set of social relationships that exists in a period of time. Historians don't simply describe a moment in time. We usually write because there is a problem in the past that we want to understand and we want to find a strategy for getting people to look at it."[1] Almost all of the characters and some of the events in "Molders of Troy" are fictional, yet as Walkowitz explains, this allowed special attention to be paid to developing important historical issues like the organization of workers and the role of labor unions in the histories of communities in the nineteenth century. The observations of historian-filmmakers can make viewers more sensitive to the creative goals of producers. Students should also consider these questions: What is it that historian-filmmakers would like viewers to learn from their films? How might that compare with the objectives of traditional scholarship?

Commercially produced historical films often distort matters of his-

[1] Barbara Abrash and Janet Sternberg, eds., *Historians and Filmmakers: Toward Collaboration* (New York, 1983), 13.

torical fact and interpretation. When commercial filmmakers, even the more responsible ones, conduct what the industry calls research, they do something very different from what a scholar does. Great attention is given to the verification and duplication of costumes, props, and nuances of language and expression. When studios promote these films by bragging about scrupulous authenticity in sets and costumes, they produce a reality effect, which like the richly detailed descriptions in a historical novel, gives the reader the aura of authenticity. In film, such authenticity of detail often masks drastic alteration of historical issues and events in the interest of maximizing entertainment values.

Some years ago, in researching the production history of the film *Drums Along the Mohawk* (1939), I was allowed access to the files at Twentieth Century Fox. In the studio library I found the bundled materials collected in the name of research for that production. There were books, pamphlets, and copied articles about the architectural style of frontier forts in the eighteenth century, detailed commentaries on costumes for Indians and farm women, and lists of appropriate furnishings for Albany manor homes and frontier log houses. In another building across the studio lot were the production files, which told a very different story. Here, in the hands of producer Darryl Zanuck, history took a backseat to dramatic storytelling. In a series of conferences with the screenwriters, Zanuck stressed repeatedly that their job was to "make entertainment," not to give America a history lesson. "We must tighten what plot we have and make it more forceful—so that we build and build to a big sustaining sock climax where we let everything go with a bang."[16] The cavalry-to-the-rescue ending Zanuck grafted onto the story provided the punch that he wanted, but historically it was pure fantasy.

Some of the so-called documentary films most often used in the history classroom present even greater challenges. Compilation films and videos made for the classroom often amount to little more than illustrated lectures, with an omniscient narrator providing all the relevant information. In the worst of these, there is little, if any, concern given to the authenticity of the footage used. A film such as *The Twisted Cross* (1956), for example, still a standard item in many educational film and video collections, raises serious concerns by shifting from actuality to dramatic footage borrowed from entertainment feature films without informing the viewer of the shifts. This structure causes the audience to presume that all the images are real and therefore provide evidence that proves the statements made in the narration. A class project might challenge students to hypothesize about the sources of footage and sound-track elements in a film like *The Twisted Cross* and

[16] *"Drums Along the Mohawk:* A Reaffirmation of American Ideals," in John E. O'Connor and Martin A. Jackson, eds., *American History/American Film* (New York, 1979), 102-103.

to consider how such observations support or detract from the message of the production.

A sequence from *Women of Summer* (1986), a documentary compilation film about the summer school for working women operated at Bryn Mawr College in the 1920s and 1930s, is also included in the video compilation. The sequence concerns response to the Sacco and Vanzetti case and consists of film footage from several sources, some of it archival footage from the 1920s and some of it recorded at a recent reunion of the women involved. The point of view here is explicit: the Sacco and Vanzetti case was one of the first public issues that moved the women to become social and political activists. The images are accompanied by the comments of a narrator and the reminiscences of one of the women who became emotionally involved in the issues at the time, and almost sixty years later was still moved to tears by the memory. Yet another element on the sound track is a song about Sacco and Vanzetti, sung powerfully by activist folksinger Holly Near. The point of view thus operates on at least three levels: the images themselves, edited to describe the experience of those who demonstrated and protested on behalf of Sacco and Vanzetti; the tearful memories of the woman at the reunion; and Holly Near's song, which draws connections between the social activism of the 1920s and that of the 1980s. As is often the case in historical documentaries, the narration and sound track are at least as important as the visual images in conveying the point of view of the film.

One additional concern about the production of historical films and docudramas is that their influence is long lasting. Unlike a historical monograph, to which another scholar may respond with an article or monograph, a film has a more permanent presence in the public mind. This longevity is accentuated, of course, when 16-mm prints or videocassettes of the film go on the market for classroom use. Once feelings about a subject have been engendered by a memorable film, they are difficult, even impossible, to counter or replace.

Commercial filmmaking and television production are first and foremost business enterprises. If a film does not turn a profit at the box office, if a television show does not win a significant audience share, few will care how well or how poorly it was produced. As with any commercial enterprise, there are institutional imperatives that drive production and inevitably influence the end result. Some are strictly commercial, such as avoiding issues so controversial or characterizations so complex that the product does not appeal to a mass audience. When a filmmaker is concerned with making a film that will sell in other countries, other interesting commercial problems arise, as in D. W. Griffith's effort in *America* (1924) to make a film on the American Revolution that would appeal to British audiences as well as American.

In some ways the demands of film are quite different from those of television. In the format of a TV miniseries, the makers of "Roots" had twelve hours to present their message, opening up opportunities a filmmaker might never dream of. Since network TV programs are seen all over the nation on the same evenings, promotional efforts can be focused on making the viewing a mass experience; much of the surprising popularity of "Roots" resulted from people discussing the program as it evolved, day after day at work and over the dinner table. On the other hand, there are specific limitations in television, such as the need to pace dramatic development around regular commercial breaks. In visual terms, there are differences too. Film lends itself to vast panoramas, while television is more a medium of close-ups and head-and-shoulder shots.

If some scholars are understandably reluctant to use films, even documentary films, to study the past, there is near common agreement on the value of such productions for an understanding of a culture's historical mentality. *The Birth of a Nation* is an intriguing document for studying Americans' perceptions of the Civil War fifty years after its end. Of course, all of the commercial imperatives and media conventions must be considered in this type of analysis as well. In most cases, the filmic interpretation of the past, like written interpretation, is influenced by contemporary issues and events. Thus, *Little Big Man* (1968) and *Soldier Blue* (1970), both ostensibly films about white America's treatment of the Indians, were largely about Vietnam, a topic too controversial for many producers to address directly at that time.

Recognizing such connections adds insight to an understanding of how a culture views both its present and its past. This is particularly true when considering the production and reception of historical films over time. Alain Resnais's documentary *Night and Fog* (1955) combines black-and-white archival footage of the Nazi concentration camps with color images taken a decade later. When first released, the film was praised for its sensitivity, but perhaps due to the proximity of the events, it was not critiqued as a historical film. Over the years it has become standard fare for many teachers struggling for ways to introduce their students to the plight of the Jews in Nazi-dominated Europe and the horrors of the Holocaust. In this context, however, it has recently been argued that the film presents a biased interpretation because it is not explicit enough in identifying the Jewishness of the victims (the narrator mentions the word Jew only once, and the word does not appear at all in the English subtitles). To bring the history of the film full circle, when Resnais was recently asked how he might explain this apparent bias, he said that it had never been his central purpose to comment on the Jews and the Holocaust. Explaining his intention to communicate a universal message about human cruelty, Resnais noted that in 1955 France was critically embroiled in Algeria. Resnais's main interest in making the film had been to warn the French against the dangers of falling into patterns of inhumanity themselves.[17] His observations reveal the film much more clearly as a document of 1955, but the film is also interesting because of the ways that it has influenced, intentionally or not, the historical perception of thousands of history classes since that time.

In evaluating and analyzing a film that purports to represent history, teachers should endeavor to whatever extent possible to apply the same general standards that they would to a traditional work of scholarship or a serious historical novel. That judgment should involve questions of content, production, and reception. Questions about content should include: Does a close analysis of the content of the film reveal a thoughtful and coherent interpretation of the historical issues and events being portrayed? How does the visual style and narrative structure of the film color its point of view? Can that interpretation be supported by the body of scholarly evidence available? For a dramatized film, to what extent were the script and the characters based on direct historical evidence and to what extent were they fictionalized? Such fictions, of course, can be appropriate and illuminating, but students should be developing some sense of where the evidence ends and fiction begins. Similarly, are the characterizations and relationships developed (for either actual or fictional characters) in tune with the historical period, or have they been modernized so that contemporary audiences would find it easier to relate to the story? For a documentary film, how is visual evidence used? Is the theme of the film presented through the information contained in the images themselves, or do the images serve only as an illustrative backdrop to a dominant voice-over commentary or narration? Are film clips from other times and places, perhaps even from theatrical films, intercut with actuality footage in a way that the viewer might mistake them for contemporary actuality footage? Does the film's research effort seem to have been limited to film sources, or are the filmmakers well-read and informed about the broader body of evidence and interpretation on the subject? If on-screen interview comments of historical participants are included, how are they used? Is it made clear that, interesting as it may be, each memory represents only one perspective, or are such memories allowed to stand as the uniting interpretive theme? Does the film indicate in any explicit way that it represents only one, or at best several, point of view, and that there might be equally acceptable alternative interpretations?

Turning to questions of production as they relate to moving-image documents as representations of history, students should ask: What can be discovered about the circumstances of the film's production and how those circumstances may have influenced production decisions? For ex-

[17] Charles Krantz, "Teaching *Night and Fog*: History and Historiography," *Film & History*, 15 (February 1985): 2-15.

ample, was the film funded in whole or in part by some organization or agency that might have had an interest in proffering one or another interpretation? Do the filmmakers bring to the project a preconceived ideological point of view? If so, is this bias stated explicitly in the film, or is there an effort to hide it or to feign objectivity? If there were historical consultants involved, what role did they play? Were they intimately involved throughout the process, or were they called in at one point simply to lend their imprimatur to the product? Were they satisfied with the results? What were the objectives of the film production? Was it purely a commercial enterprise in which people might have been less hesitant to sacrifice historical veracity for audience appeal? Was it made with a specific audience in mind? Did the filmmaker have any previous experience in historical filmmaking by which to gauge the level of sensitivity or care for detail? How might the goals and purposes of the film compare with the objectives of traditional scholarship?

Finally, students should ask questions about reception: How was the film received? What type of distribution did it receive, and how did audiences respond to the film? Specifically, how did specialists in the historical subject area evaluate the film's portrayal?[18] Were there different versions of the film produced at different times for different audiences, and how did these changes alter responses? If the film is not a recent production, how may audience reactions to it have changed over time? How might these various responses improve understanding and appreciation of the meaning of the film?

Framework Two: Moving-image documents as evidence for social and cultural history. Most teachers who use commercially produced feature films or television programs in the classroom have sought to involve their students in analyzing the social and cultural values present in them. The field is rich for studying changing attitudes toward race, gender, urban or rural lifestyles, and scores of other issues. Film and television also offer many possibilities for the study of popular culture. While traditional history study lets students know what people in the past knew or believed, film and television study can aid in understanding what made them laugh or cry.

Theatrical and entertainment productions are not the only ones that relate to social and cultural values. The documentary filmmaker's decision about what films to make and how to make them, and the television news producer's decision about what stories to cover and how to cover them, are equally relevant. Some of the richest documents for future historians to study for an understanding of today's culture will be television commercials.

[18] Many historical journals have begun to publish such reviews on a regular basis, and there are two historical journals that specialize in media: *Film & History* and *The Historical Journal of Film, Radio and Television.*

Many communications scholars have taken a social science approach to the measurement and analysis of what they term cultural indicators in the media. As appealing as such a straightforward approach might appear, in the context of historical scholarship there are specific methodological concerns that such an analysis invariably brings into play. There is the danger, for example, of suggesting to students an oversimple concept of what constitutes culture. When teachers encourage students to concentrate on single objects as cultural indicators (books, films, or material objects), they run the risk of characterizing culture as being too stable and comprehensive. In contrast, modern culture is never monolithic. There are always important differences of class, race, and gender that must be considered. Moreover, tastes, values, and attitudes are always in flux, and different groups in the society are likely to be ahead or behind in that ongoing process.

When considering the history of the 1920s or 1930s, there is no more lively expression of the culture of the period than its films, but there is the danger that the films may skew historical perception. Unless the variety and complexity of popular culture are constantly stressed, students will be easily misguided by the films' very vitality. Students may mistakenly assume that because the films of the 1920s and 1930s are the most vital elements of that time for them, the same was true for people living at the time. The naive comment of one student suggests the unspoken conclusions of many: "Films had more impact on society in the 1920s than they do in the 1980s because today there are so many more interesting things going on."

In one common classroom approach, film can be used as a convincing illustration or reinforcement of the social and cultural values current in a period under study. Teachers may suggest to the students that the values and prejudices inherent in the film correspond with the values and prejudices of the broader culture. Thus, a class studying the Progressive Era in American history might view a film such as Griffith's *A Corner in Wheat* (1909), in addition to discussing the Populist and Progressive attitudes and political beliefs of the period. There is no more effective document for reinforcing an understanding of the social and economic values of the time, contrasting country and city, rich and poor, capital and labor. Moreover, a close study of this fourteen-minute film (included in the video compilation) helps to reveal the intellectual discourse of the period directly through the unique narrative form of the film, which is similar in structure to the muckraking literature of the period. *A Corner in Wheat* is short enough for a class to study closely; segmenting, analyzing specific shots and sequences, and viewing the film a second time can all take place in the same class period. Such a lesson would illuminate the psychology of the Progressive Era at least as well as a discussion of any reading from Upton Sinclair or Lincoln Steffens, while teaching important visual literacy skills.

A film like *The Green Pastures* (1936) reveals the racial stereotypes of its era. In addition, the structure of the film creates a fantasy world in which its all-black cast can react with one another. (In the context of the actual society of the time, the main concern would more likely have been how blacks would relate to whites.) Similarly, Charlie Chaplin's *Modern Times* (1936) is anything but a factual representation of industrial life in thirties America, though it clearly points up some of the economic and social ironies that many people were sensitive to at the time. Students can learn from moving-image documents by looking for ways the emotions and values evoked by a document might correspond to aspects of the society and culture already known. Both students and teachers should be aware, however, that the full analysis of a moving image as a social or cultural document demands more in-depth research.

Every film or television show has a production history that might radically transform its value as a document of the past. As with any major undertaking, often a film does not turn out the way it was originally intended. Over the months or years necessary to bring a film to the screen, the budget may have been cut, one of the actors may have died, or any number of other factors may have intervened to transform the attitudes and values addressed in the film. Understanding the production background of a film such as *The Birth of a Race* (1917), included in the video compilation, demonstrates how production variables can influence the resulting film. The project, begun by a Chicago-based black production company headed by Booker T. Washington as an answer to *The Birth of a Nation*, was at first intended to trace the development of civilization through the contributions of blacks. When the company went bankrupt, it was taken over by whites, who changed the thrust of the project while retaining a liberal point of view. At the start of World War I there were pressures to add still another message to the already compromised intent. The guide to the video compilation contains copies of manuscript records, which document some of these transformations and underline the importance of not presuming that the significance of a film as a social and cultural document can be understood completely from what appears on the screen. Sometimes understanding why certain images were not included in the final version of a film can be even more illuminating. To gain this understanding, more and more historians are seeking out the archival "paper trail" that documents the production process. Teachers should be aware of such scholarship before they invite a class to hypothesize about the meaning of a film.

The study of reception is also extremely important when working with moving images as social and cultural documents. After all, the values and attitudes that historians seek to understand were never inherent to the moving image itself; they were in the minds of the people who saw the film and responded to it, sometimes unconsciously. The "Daisy Spot," the famous sixty-second television commercial from the

1964 Johnson presidential campaign (included in the video compilation), demonstrates this. Students who see the commercial today may have a hard time understanding the controversy that led to the spot being pulled after airing only once on TV. Producer Tony Schwartz explains that the piece was important less because of what it explicitly stated and more because of the frame of mind of the people who saw and heard it. By allowing President Johnson to express abhorrence of the potential for nuclear annihilation, the piece was designed to focus viewers' attention on the widely perceived notion that Republican candidate Barry Goldwater would be more inclined to deploy nuclear weapons. Without stating this in any way, the commercial concentrated voters' thoughts on perhaps the greatest liability of Johnson's opponent, because those ideas were already in people's minds. That the commercial was televised only once does not diminish its value as a barometer of the public mind, but reading that gauge must be performed with some care if students are to learn some important lessons about the media and politics, both in the past and in the present.

It is important that scholars and teachers be aware of the complexity of audience response and remain ever-conscious of the broader social context in which past audiences made sense of what they saw. Thomas Cripps has shown this clearly in the case of Stepin Fetchit, who made a successful career for himself over several decades by playing the stereotypical role of a hapless black clown. While white liberal audiences may have been embarrassed and dismayed, in black neighborhoods, where Fetchit's name was often displayed above the title on movie marquees, he was often seen as a hero for having made a successful career in the movies and for earning enough money to live the life of a movie star.[1]

The study of films of propaganda and persuasion is best done in the framework of moving-image documents as evidence for social and cultural history. Filmmakers in Russia (Eisenstein, Kuhlesov, Pudovkin), Britain (Grierson, Elton, Wright), and Germany (Riefenstahl) were the first to recognize the potential of the moving image as a propaganda device, but others, including American filmmakers, were not far behind. Students should understand the persuasive power of the broadly interpretive Russian feature films of the 1920s (*Battleship Potemkin, Ten Days That Shook the World, Mother, Earth*) as well as the propagandistic British social documentaries of the 1930s (*Industrial Britain, Housing Problems*) and the racist and political propaganda of the Nazis (*Olympia, Triumph of the Will*). A classroom project to identify the propaganda elements, visual and otherwise, in films like these would involve students directly in some of the most pertinent issues of both political history and visual communication.

---

[1] For further insight into the complexities of race and moving images, see Thomas Cripps, *Slow Fade to Black: The Negro in American Film* (New York, 1977).

As with the "Daisy Spot," the values and attitudes present in the population are key to understanding how propaganda works. The video compilation includes *Für Uns* (1937), a Nazi Party film focusing on the anniversary of the 1923 Beer Hall Putsch in which sixteen Nazis had been killed. Both the guide to the video compilation and the voice-over commentary by historian Robert Herzstein explain how the film used formal structure, visual language, narration, and music to play on themes rooted deep in German culture. The film urges viewers to associate in their minds the sixteen Nazi "martyrs" with the two million Germans who died in World War I, resurrecting the nationalistic spirit of the German people and urging them to unite behind Hitler. Since *Für Uns* is only fourteen minutes long, a teacher might want to screen the film once, discuss it with the class, and then view it a second time with Herzstein's commentary on the second sound track.

In terms of content, the analysis of a film or video production as historical artifact for the study of social and cultural history should give special attention to the values represented in the narrative structure and the style assumed in establishing the composition and mise-en-scène than to the accuracy or inaccuracy of the images. Students should ask the following questions: Do the social and cultural concepts represented relate to other known aspects of the society and culture of the period? Does the film or television production lead or trail behind other media in representing those ideas? Are there interpretive biases not necessarily explicit in the narration, dialogue, or surface message of the production, but hidden in its visual language? Are there aspects of culture not easily perceived in other types of artifacts, such as patterns of movement, gesture, facial expression, and body language?

When considering questions of production, special attention should be given to the purpose of the production. If the film is strictly a work of commercial entertainment, it can be assumed that the producers were trying to strike existing chords in the society and culture of the time (as the producers recognized them). This sort of assumption may suffice for an analysis of correspondence, but research scholars will want to try to confirm such judgments by studying any production records that might be available. The commercial purpose of an entertainment production might be moderated by a particular point of view, for example, a producer's desire to encourage improved race relations. But a big-budget, studio-produced entertainment film involves the input of many collaborators. The concept of the auteur may have its place, but such an analysis is particularly vulnerable with large-scale commercial productions. Of course, there are productions that are dominated by a single point of view, as in an independently produced art film or a television commercial for a political campaign. In each case, access to production records is sure to improve the insights that can be drawn. When the production history of a film is inaccessible, students may hypothesize on the motives and rationale of the filmmaker, but they should remember that a hypothesis is different from a conclusion based on a close analysis of the documented evidence.

Perhaps the most important area in defining the social and cultural relevance of a moving-image document is reception. Film reviews are a good place to start, though it must be remembered that the reviewer for *The New York Times* does not necessarily get the same message from a film as the reviewer from Richmond or Kansas City, and that none of those reviewers are necessarily in touch with the desires of the nation's moviegoers. There are other types of paper evidence, such as preview response cards, advertising press books, and letters to the editor, but in making this kind of analysis the gaps will almost always be greater than the documented spaces. In bridging these gaps, one might turn to theoretical approaches to reception analysis, but such approaches are always well served by incorporating as much solid evidence as may be available. There were many individual or group responses to any film, and different racial, ethnic, gender, or political groups may have perceived the production differently or recognized different meanings implicit within it. By investigating the events and topics covered in the newspapers, magazines, and other vehicles of popular culture during the weeks and months that the film was in release, some part of the context in which viewers saw the production can be established. In whatever other ways possible, students should try to "get inside the skin" of the viewers. Finally, while a film need not have been a smashing popular success or a television show in the top ten of the weekly Neilsen ratings to be of value as a document, a production that strikes a chord with an audience is at least some measure of its relevance as a social or cultural document.

Framework Three: Moving-image documents as evidence for historical fact. Many of those who use film in their history classes today rely on it to convey a body of facts. This is the approach taken by the makers of most films and videotapes commercially produced for the classroom. In addition to the convenience these films provide, studies suggest that, combined with lecture and discussion, their use may reinforce knowledge and improve recall. Most classroom screenings, however, rely on the students' internalization of the surface messages of the film. The teacher hopes that they will take in the information that the filmmaker wants them to take in. Rather than being challenged to think and analyze, students are too often reinforced in the passive viewing habits they have learned watching their televisions at home.

In factual footage, such as the Zapruder film of the Kennedy assassination, the factual data provided in the image itself can be unexpectedly informative if the viewer undertakes a truly active reading. By counting the frames of the Zapruder film, the investigators of the Warren Commission were able to establish the precise amount of time between the shots fired. The Zapruder film is so memorable because its factual testimony was so unusual. The very nature of film and television images, the limits of point of view within a shot, and the opportunities for misrepresentation in the editing process make most film notoriously unreliable as a factual resource, but unedited factual images like the Zapruder film offer unique material for analysis.

Newsreel and television archives contain the raw material for historical scholarship, more than any other collections of moving images. Newsreel images can add a dimension to the study of many subjects. Among the most important are newsreels that offer the kinds of information that can only be perceived visually. Newsreel images of Franklin Delano Roosevelt, for example, like photographs of Abraham Lincoln, show how his face aged during his years in office. What only the moving images can demonstrate, however, is how Roosevelt's handicap made his physical movement more and more troublesome as the years passed. Like any film, however, newsreels were subject to editing, and all the factual film shot was seldom used in the final version of a newsreel. The message of factual images can therefore be altered, affecting viewers' perception of the message. The way FDR was protected by the newsreels is illustrated by the Movietone News outtakes included in the video compilation.

Television news as factual resource can be equally problematic. It is especially difficult to find tapes of national television news coverage before 1968, when the Vanderbilt Television News Archive began regular taping of the three networks. Local news coverage is all but impossible to study in any comprehensive way because of a lack of systematic taping. At present, there are efforts under way to preserve some local news programming and archive it for scholars' future reference. But even if access were easily available (as hopefully it some day may be), scholars must remain sensitive to the limitations of TV news as factual resource. While at first glance it may seem that the images are inherently more factual than written accounts in newspapers and magazines, moving-image scholars must remember that all images are interpretive as well. On the other hand, as Daniel Boorstin established so convincingly in *The Image: Or What Happened to the American Dream* (New York, 1962), today's news is largely made up of "pseudo-events." In a world driven by public opinion, what "really happened" may not matter as much as what was reported and how.

Television is reality for masses of people, and in an important sense, analytical problems of reception notwithstanding, this transforms TV broadcasts into historical fact. The video compilation includes a selection from the CBS Evening News that illustrates this point. When CBS made the decision to focus especially on one statement made by Edward Kennedy in his campaign for the 1980 Democratic presidential nomination, they transformed it into a much more significant event than it otherwise might have been. The most important point to make with students in an analysis of television news as evidence for historical fact is that, although most electronic journalism is accurate, within the inevitable limitations of the medium, film and television images should not be presumed to be more reliable sources of information simply because they are visual, that is, because they make all viewers in some way eyewitnesses. Indeed, it is important that people be able to trust media-based reporting in a media-dominated society. That trust, however, should be based on a clear comprehension of the conventions of the medium and the ways it communicates its information, not on a naive belief that the camera makes viewers eyewitnesses to events.

At Columbia University a current project takes Soviet television news off a satellite and studies it for insight into both Soviet policy and public awareness. Because there is a degree of speculation involved in this kind of study, scholars must take care when they generalize about audience perceptions. Aside from the absence of an institutionalized opposition (immediate critical analysis of a presidential speech, for example), why should it be presumed that Soviet audiences are any more naive than American audiences in blindly accepting their government's interpretations of issues and events?

Historians can make effective use of certain documentary films in their entirety as factual resources, although each reference should include a careful analysis of the filmmaker's point of view and a verification through other sources of the facts percieved. Robert Flaherty's *Nanook of the North* (1922) is a film that is probably unreliable for specific facts (many of the scenes were purposely enacted or reenacted for the sake of the cameras), but is wonderful for an overall impression— one perceptive view—of what native American life was like in the Great North. The films of Frederick Wiseman also provide several interesting examples. Wiseman produced an extended series of cinema verité documentaries that closely examine American institutions as diverse as an Anglican seminary and a downtown police department. The historian of education, for example, might very profitably view Wiseman's *High School* (1968) to get a feeling for the dynamics of the American high school in the 1960s. The military historian might benefit as much from studying Wiseman's *Basic Training* (1971), as would the historian of American consumer practices from *The Store* (1983), a close-up look at Dallas's Neiman-Marcus department store. Of all the institutions Wiseman has studied with his camera, perhaps the most interesting is the mental hospital profiled in *Titicut Follies* (1967) because there are so few visual documents like it. Historians must be careful to avoid accepting Wiseman's view as more truthful than another source just because it is constructed of actuality footage. Conversely, a historian who wrote on this subject without attention to Wiseman's factual insights would clearly be missing something. Peter Davis's six-part documentary series

Middletown (1982) should become a factual resource on the early 1980s in the same way as the Lynds' famous study of Muncie, Indiana (minus the visual dimension) has for generations served as a factual resource for social historians of the 1920s.

Teachers should continue using film and video as a shorthand way to present factual information to a class, but because of the special concerns of content that arise when using moving images as factual sources, students should be made aware that the information imparted is no more or less reliable because it is reinforced with pictures. At least some attention should be paid in the classroom to teaching students how the form and style of visual images, and especially the patterns and conventions of editing, raise questions about the reliability of film or television as proof that events happened in one way or another, or that they happened at all.

When considering questions of production, it is important to inquire into the purposes and biases of the filmmakers and camera operators that may have led them to photograph, select, or edit footage in a particular way. In some cases, as with news film in a totalitarian country or with propaganda documentaries, the intent of the filmmaker may be the central question for analysis. There is considerable literature on the institution of television news and the ways decisions are made regarding what is reported and how. Students therefore should understand how media conventions influence the information they receive.

Factual analysis of news film, in conjunction with press reports and other sources, allows some estimation of what the public knew, or thought it knew, at any particular time. It is important, however, not to presume that the audience is totally naive and impressionable. Scholarship has raised important questions about the extent to which populations are taken in by propaganda, especially when characterized by blatantly falsified reports. How much does the public, even in a free society, accept the interpretation of events presented in the news?

Finally, the conditions of the reception of television news present particular problems. As news programs assume more of the trappings of entertainment programs, and program flow is carefully designed by specialists in the industry to lead audiences from one program to the next, it is unclear what influence such media context has on the public's perception of issues and events. Considering such problems with a class should help to make the students more critical viewers.

Framework Four: Moving-image documents as evidence for the history of film and television. The art forms of film and television (closely related but significantly different from one another) and the industries that produce them are arguably among the most historically significant twentieth-century institutional subjects available for study. While the impact that media have had on culture cannot be proved in a specific or clinical way, it is safe to say that moving-image media rank with other such hard-to-quantify forces as the factory system and the automobile. The history of film and television, therefore, deserves to be studied and taught in its own right, and there is as much reason for this to be taught in the history department as in departments of communications, cinema studies, or English. There have been a few valuable and widely read studies that have tried to lay the groundwork for such activity including Garth Jowett's *Film: The Democratic Art* (Boston, 1976) and Robert Sklar's *Movie-Made America* (New York, 1975). There is also the *Historical Journal of Film, Radio and Television*, which specializes in work by historians about the history of the media. But there has yet to be a recognition of the importance of the institutional history of film as part of the larger mainstream of history. It is one thing for an author to refer to a film or to the popular image of Hollywood to help characterize a period, but it is quite another to recognize the importance of self-regulation and censorship within the American film industry as a characteristic in American economic life. Of all the textbook treatments of American history available, none does real justice to the mass media as an industry, an art form, or a force in modern civilization.

There has been a continuing and appropriate distinction made between what has commonly been known as film history—the popular and somewhat nostalgic tale-telling about the public and private lives of the Hollywood stars and their studios—and the more serious analytical work of traditionally trained historians. It is wrong to presume, however, that historians are the only ones who were dissappointed with what passed for film history. Although fan biographies and pictorial histories continue to be published, there has been a significant transformation in the practice of film history over the past decade, as specialists trained in cinema studies have developed a substantial body of scholarship on the historical analysis of film and television. Two recent books of particular importance to those teaching the history of film and television are David Bordwell, Janet Staiger, and Kristin Thompson's *The Classical Hollywood Cinema: Film Style and Mode of Production to 1960* (New York, 1985) and Douglas Gomery and Robert Allen's *Film History: Theory and Practice* (New York, 1985). Reading these books should be an important step in raising the consciousness of any history teacher undertaking a course in film history. Bridging the gap necessary to intelligently read historical articles published in such important cinema journals as *Wide Angle, Cinema Journal, Screen,* or *Quarterly Review of Film Studies* will be easier for those historians who are conversant with recent trends in the philosophy of history. The work of thinkers such as Hayden White and Michel Foucault have been central to these new historians who were trained first in cinema studies.

Art history is another field that should inform historical investigation of film and television. There are striking resemblances between the new directions in art history over the past decade and the development of serious scholarship for film as social and cultural artifact. One basic theme in art history has been stimulated by the recognition that styles in painting, sculpture, architecture, and other plastic arts, rather than being strictly formalistic extensions of earlier styles, are invariably related to other forces in the society. This can be readily seen in such studies as Samuel Edgerton's *Renaissance Rediscovery of Linear Perspective* (New York, 1975), which demonstrates in detail how the new style in drawing came to represent a visual metaphor for many aspects of the contemporary culture of Florence, from the increasing rationality in banking and commerce to the growing political dominance of the Medici family. This is the obverse side of the framework for analyzing moving-image documents as evidence for social and cultural history. Films can be studied for what they can tell about the social and cultural values of the time, but people primarily interested in the close historical analysis of a film itself, or a genre of films, should be using social and cultural history to help them understand the film as a work of art.

One particularly interesting avenue of recent film history research has centered on the founding and early development of the industry. In addition to tracing the invention of the technology and the establishment of the production companies, research has focused on the creation of new narrative and nonnarrative structures, new ways to tell stories made possible by the plasticity of space and time in film. Edwin S. Porter's *The Life of an American Fireman* (1902) provides what may be a unique example of such a process. Most prints of this short film that exist today are based on one that was restored several decades ago. Unsure of the original order of the shots in the climax of the film, the restorers put the shots together in a way that made sense to them. They intercut the footage so that the point of view shifted freely from exterior to interior and back again, maintaining a continuity of time in telling the story of the rescue of a woman and child from a burning building. Research has recently established that the original film first presented one long interior shot showing the entire drama of the firemen breaking into a smoky room and carrying the woman and child down the ladder. The camera then switched to the outside of the building to show the same events repeated a second time from that point of view. For these early filmmakers, continuity of space was more important than continuity of time; it would have been more disconcerting for turn-of-the-century audiences to have the camera move from one vantage point to another than it was to have the same events repeated. The development of new ways to tell stories meant that spectators had to learn new ways to make meaning from stories as well.[20]

[20] See the video compilation and guide.

The field of film history has been radically transformed and professionalized in the last two decades. What might have been acceptable as a film history course fifteen years ago simply will not suffice in the face of so much new scholarship. Any teacher who undertook to offer a film history course today that jumped from twenties comedies to thirties social realism and forties *film noir* by simply discussing the films themselves, or using a popular survey such as Arthur Knight's *The Liveliest Art* (New York, 1957) as a text, would be doing a disservice to the students. There are different opinions about the relative value of various theoretical orientations, but one cannot responsibly teach the history of film or television today without careful attention to institutional organizations, economic imperatives, technological developments, patterns of spectatorship, and a host of other factors. Most important, one cannot present a film as an artifact in the history of an industry or art form without engaging in close analysis. The contexts of content, production, and reception must be filled out as in the traditional manuscript research in which all historians are trained. There is a growing body of scholarship based on this kind of research that will offer teachers of film history the materials they need for designing the more substantial courses that the field demands today. (For examples, see the study guide materials on *The Birth of a Race, A Corner in Wheat, The Return of Martin Guerre,* and *The Plow That Broke the Plains* that accompany the video compilation.)

Studying the content of a moving-image document in the context of the history of the industry and art form of moving images involves recognizing that a careful viewing of the films themselves provides important evidence for film history. Until recent years, most historians of popular film have been content with summarizing plots and general stylistic elements in the films they discussed, most of which were recognized as masterpieces and seen most widely on 16-mm rental prints and on TV. This has at least in part been due to the inaccessibility of film archives and the special projectors or viewing tables necessary for close visual analysis. The video revolution and the growing availability of videodisk technology is changing this, as more and more titles become available in formats that invite close analysis. The video compilation designed to accompany this publication has been produced in videodisk (as well as videotape) to encourage the deeper analysis that disk technology facilitates.

Just as art historians need to understand the background of a painter's work and the techniques of line and brush, so film historians require an understanding of the mode of moving-image production. Today, serious film history cannot be conducted without investigating the archival record of the industry to understand how the production process of a specific film worked. Current scholarship begins to provide this kind of background.

The study of moviegoing is a part of social and cultural history, but in a slightly different way it also reflects the consumption side of industrial history. Students should ask: How were the expectations of viewers influenced by the promotional efforts of the studio or TV network? How much was dependent on matters other than the film or TV program itself, such as the offering of air conditioning, the sumptuous design of movie palaces, or the use of videocassette recorders to "time shift" certain programs for later viewing? Such factors cannot be forgotten in the teaching of film and television history.

Strategies for the Classroom

Teachers use films to convey information (often for class review), to sensitize students to a past era, and to stimulate discussion. Each of these approaches can be enhanced when applied more thoughtfully. Those who use film to convey information should do so sparingly and should caution students to accept such information only after it has been verified through other sources. Students must be reminded that information derived from moving images is no more inherently truthful than information gained from reading or class lecture, despite what they "saw with their own eyes." Teachers who use film to sensitize students to a past era—showing *The Return of Martin Guerre* to make the life of the sixteenth-century French peasant more real—should take care not to reinforce habits of passive viewing. Certainly every lesson cannot focus on production background and visual language, but at least one lesson each term should help keep students aware that the feelings they get from watching a film are not coincidental. Students will then become more cognizant of the powerful tools filmmakers may use to move their audience. In the classroom it is particularly appropriate for history teachers, at least on occasion, to approach moving images as historical documents, reinforcing concepts of historical thinking while teaching visual literacy.

The central purpose of this book is to encourage and assist teachers in incorporating a few more critical viewing lessons into their otherwise traditional history classes. Those interested in a more expansive approach should be aware that in a number of high schools and colleges, elective courses have been completely structured around the study of history through film and television. A teacher could easily devote an entire semester to the concerns expressed in this book. A college class could spend several productive weeks working through a textbook on the critical analysis of moving images. Models also exist for courses that concentrate on Hollywood feature film, documentary and news film, or film and photography.[21] A semester-long concentration on film and history study would allow an in-depth analysis of a number of different

---

[21] In some ways the critical reading of photographs can be even more challenging than film and TV. See Susan Sontag, *On Photography* (New York, 1973) and Roland Barthes, *Camera Lucida: Reflections on Photography* (New York, 1981).

films, but the number of films addressed should be decided conservatively. Courses structured around one feature film a week seldom leave enough time for close study. In certain circumstances, it might not be unreasonable to spend two or three weeks on a single film, studying its content, re-viewing and discussing particular scenes, comparing the film with other film treatments of the period, tracing the film's production history through a reading and analysis of primary or secondary sources, examining its reception, including an analysis of the broader context of popular culture at the time the film was originally released, and applying each of the four frameworks for inquiry.

In a film and history course for college juniors and seniors at New Jersey Institute of Technology, I have devoted this kind of attention, for example, to *The Plow That Broke the Plains*, spending four eighty-minute class periods (two weeks of class time) on a twenty-eight-minute film, with rewarding results. The class began by reading sections of Donald Worster's *Dust Bowl: The Southern Plains in the 1930s* (New York, 1979) and viewing *The Plow* with the shorter ending (the way the film was distributed by the government between 1936 and 1940, and again after 1962 when the film was cleared once more for educational distribution). On the blackboard we broke the film down into its seven major sequences, so that the class could concentrate on individual images and discuss how they worked as symbols in the film. Because *The Plow* was produced by the government and is free of any copyright restrictions, I did not hesitate to make a series of slides from the screen for close analysis in class.[22] Moreover, I made videotape copies of the seven major sequences of the film, which students could borrow to study on their own (all but two or three had video recorders at home). The class was divided into seven groups, and each group was assigned one sequence for an in-depth analysis. At the close of the first eighty-minute class, we viewed a dozen of the slides that depicted some of the visual symbols in the film. The class was given a packet of photocopies of contemporary reviews of the film and manuscript papers[23] relating to its production, and told to read them by the next class.

When the class met again three days later, the students could not understand how the film they had seen and discussed could have caused the controversy that was evident from the documents they had read. Could the congressmen who had been so upset about *The Plow* in the

[22] There are attachments that will allow direct copying of a 16-mm frame with a 35-mm camera, but I have been able to produce adequate copies for classroom use by setting up a camera on a tripod next to the projector in a dark room, stopping the action of the projector, and simply snapping pictures off the screen. Teachers must be aware of the limitations, but there are situations in which the making of slides in this manner for classroom reference may be considered fair use under the copyright law. Your school should have a general policy regarding fair use. If not, you should urge them to develop one that includes film and video.

[23] Some of these papers are included in the guide to the video compilation.

1930s have been looking at the same film? At this point, I showed them the didactic pro-New Deal epilogue that was originally attached to the film and tried to impress on them the importance of verifying the completeness of any document they would analyze. In an effort to discover why and how the epilogue was removed, the class discussed the extent and impact of the dust bowl and why it happened; Republican and Democratic politics in the 1930s; the state of agriculture in the United States in the thirties and the varying ideas people had about how to respond to the plight of the farmers; and the nature of the New Deal and how it was reflected in the film. The class based their discussion in part on what they had been assigned to read in Worster's book. Because Worster presents a rather pointed interpretation, arguing that the dust bowl was the result of the same capitalist values that had brought on the economic depression, part of the discussion considered alternative points of view.

The third class period devoted to *The Plow* began with a review of what had been discovered about the content, production, and reception of the film. The students were then challenged to consider how the film might be infused with different meanings, applying each of the four frameworks for inquiry. First, they discussed how the film lends itself to analysis as historical interpretation. *The Plow* presents an especially simplistic interpretation of the economic background that led to the plight of the plains farmer. After farmers had applied new technology and geared up for wartime production, peace brought overproduction and falling prices. But even in the 1930s it was understood that the economic problems involved were much more complex; the film makes no mention of the tenancy problem, for example. By stressing the environmental dimension of the farmers' troubles, the film does lay the rationale for more active government planning for agricultural development, but it avoids a fuller critique of either technological methods or the capitalist system.

Second, the class analyzed the film as a document of social and cultural history. Students recognized the obvious images of social and cultural interest in the film, such as the migrants seeking a place where they could begin to put together new lives for themselves. The class understood that in this context there was less concern with the factual accuracy of the images than with the social and cultural values the film sought to touch in its audience. Camera angles and editing were seen as important for the ways they characterized individuals and issues, helping spectators unconsciously to develop the point of view the producers intended (the slides were helpful again here). The filmmaker, Pare Lorentz, was clearly attempting to create sympathy in the audience for people who had been victimized. The farmers of the plains had been brought there by very basic American social and cultural values. Once settled, the unpredictabilities of the economic system, combined with the vagaries of the environment, shaped their lives. A more biting social critic might have sought to deflate widely professed American ideals as empty rhetoric or as opiate for the otherwise ill-informed masses, but Lorentz did not go this far. Rather, his film suggested that the system could be made sound again and the values reaffirmed under the leadership of FDR and the enlightened policies of agencies such as the Resettlement Administration.

Third, the class discussed the reliability of *The Plow* as a resource for the facts it reported. They had read about people in the 1930s who had challenged the factual accuracy of the film. In addition, they were made aware that the compilation filmmakers who repeatedly return to *The Plow* in search of footage on the 1930s seldom if ever question the validity of the images. Although individual shots from the film may provide visual verification for the written record in much the same way as still photographs of the time, using such images to get an idea of the enormity of the dust storms or some more intimate sense of what they were like requires special attention to the photographic decisions made—at what angles were pictures shot, what kinds of lenses or filters were used, what film speed—each of which might unknowingly influence the viewers' perceptions of what actually appeared before the camera. Moreover, for images to be used as evidence, it must be clear that they were not staged and that they represent exactly what they purport to represent. In short, the class was helped to see that although *The Plow* is commonly used as a factual source on the dust bowl and the problems of the rural depression, such reference is frought with difficulty from the historian's point of view.

Finally, the class considered how *The Plow* could be studied as an important artifact in the history of documentary film and the subsequent making of documentary films by the United States government. The production of *The Plow* and Lorentz's later film, *The River* (1937), led to the establishment of a new agency, the United States Film Service, with Lorentz at its head. The administrators of the service, like the promoters of *The Plow*, struggled against political opponents until 1940, when a congressional committee forced the shutdown of the agency and the end of distribution of *The Plow* until 1962, when distribution was again permitted in recognition of the importance of the film for students of the medium.

By the fourth class period (at the end of the second week), the students were ready to discuss the work they had done on their own. They had been asked to analyze and evaluate the effectiveness of the interpretation presented in each of the major sequences and to include analyses of specific shots and specific editing transitions, with explanations about how the creative use of these visual elements, as well as the sound track, either contributed to or detracted from the message that the filmmaker was trying to convey.[24] This last class period on *The Plow* centered on discussing once again the seven major sequences of the film, with extensive references to the students' own observations about how the visual and aural elements of the film helped to accomplish the overall purpose of the production.

This history-through-film course took a similarly in-depth approach to *The Return of Martin Guerre.* The class read Natalie Zemon Davis's book of the same title (Cambridge, Mass., 1983) before they saw the film. Discussion of the film centered on the nature of history and how the creative demands of the moving-image medium challenged traditional ways of representing the past. The class began by considering the ways the intent of the filmmakers, necessarily concerned about entertaining an audience and turning a profit, differed from the more altruistic concern of the historian for expanding understanding of sixteenth-century French society. The students then considered how these different goals may have influenced the film presentation, in which important details of the story were collapsed or deleted and the characterizations simplified. The book opens with the explanation that the story is one of imposture. Throughout it shows the complexities of Bertrande's character: she is a woman capable of plotting to trick the entire community into thinking that the man who "returns" is the real Martin Guerre, yet concerned enough with protecting her own interests and those of her children to bring the legal indictment against him. On the other hand, because the film is tied to the conventions of romance and mystery movies, there was strong reason to neither suggest the potential disloyalty of the woman (breaking the spell of the romance) nor reveal the solution to the mystery (the real nature of the imposture) until the end of the film, when all of the suspense value had been spent.

The Return of Martin Guerre is a film rich in historical mise-en-scène. The research devoted to settings, costumes, and props as well as to language, music, and characterization make it wonderfully effective in evoking the texture of sixteenth-century life. The questions raised in class discussion led the students to consider the relative suitability of film and television for developing such detail in the way things looked, in contrast to the suitability of print for describing people's thoughts and feelings. The class was also assigned to read Davis' interview on the making of the film in *Film & History,* in which she discussed how the questions raised in creating the mise-en-scène for the movie challenged her to think differently about historical questions and led her to new insights about the past.[25]

The Return of Martin Guerre opens with a narrator's statement to

[24] The appendix to this book includes a sample of the class assignment and the information sheets provided for the analysis of shot and editing transitions.

[25] Ed Benson, "Martin Guerre, The Historian and The Filmmakers: An Interview With Natalie Zemon Davis," *Film & History,* 13 (September 1983): 49-65.

the effect that it is a true story. As Davis asks in her commentary on the video compilation, what does such a claim to truth mean? In what ways and to what extent can any film be true to history? The class recognized how such a claim could confuse and mislead viewers. The film required a second viewing for students to understand that the person in the film who says that the story is true is the judge whose published account provides the fullest evidence for the story. The class was able to note that the film could at least have indicated more clearly that the story was true to one person's account. More importantly, they came to better understand that every work of history represents an interpretation or point of view, and that there might be alternative narrative structures that would allow a more thoughtful approach to historical representation in film. One option might be based on the model of the Japanese film *Roshamon* (1950), in which the same event is repeated several times through the eyes of different observers.

Few teachers are likely to be in a situation where this kind of comprehensive strategy for teaching *The Plow* or *The Return of Martin Guerre* would be appropriate. However, part of the analysis might prove valuable to many teachers in very different contexts. For example, while most teachers might not want to survey all four frameworks of inquiry in studying *The Plow*, they could have their students consider the types of questions most appropriate to one selected framework. Care has been taken in this essay and in the video compilation to provide examples of shorter films that lend themselves to integration into regular history classes. It is important that the films the teacher chooses for close analysis have been researched and written about in terms of their content, production, and reception. For the vast majority of films, a "paper trail" either does not exist or has not yet been treated in published scholarship, but there are scores of films that have been studied on the basis of such archival sources. The screenplays to hundreds of feature films have been published in book series, such as the critical editions of Warner Brothers screenplays from the University of Wisconsin Press; in collected volumes, such as Sam Thomas's *Best American Screenplays* (New York, 1986); or summarized in such useful guides as Leonard Leff's *Film Plots: Scene-by-Scene Narrative Outlines for Feature Film Study,* vol. 1 (Ann Arbor, 1983).

Films or television programs to be treated in class as historical documents should be chosen at least in part according to the accessibility of production and reception information. If there are pressing reasons to utilize a film for which no background and contextual data is available, it is still important to keep matters of background and context in mind. Tentative interpretations are possible, of course, and may be provocative as devices for students, but it should always be made clear that no full determination about the overall historical significance or insight to be drawn from a moving-image production can be made in the absence of such information.

There is good reason, for example, for using some of the recognized classics like *Citizen Kane* (1941). In twenty years of teaching college history students I have never found a class where more than a few had ever seen this film, and only a handful had looked at it critically. There are now wonderful resources for the close study of this film, including the published screenplay, Robert Carringer's recent volume on the *The Making of "Citizen Kane"* (Berkeley, 1985), and the release of a CAV videodisk edition of the film, which permits flexibility in studying and comparing individual scenes (the disk even includes the advertising materials developed by RKO to sell the film and a large collection of production stills). The materials, especially the visual, on *Citizen Kane* are extraordinary, but there are scores of other feature films that have been fully researched. There are also good sources for information on the production and reception of at least some documentary films, newsreels, and television news. For designing a lesson in critical analysis, therefore, rather than starting with film catalogs to find the moving-image materials for a class, teachers should look first at the books and journals of film scholarship to identify film and video materials about which they can readily find documented information on content, production, and reception.

Teachers must be careful not to use films for the purpose of manipulating their students' perceptions. There are good film and video resources on controversial issues in recent history, films that when screened in class would leave the students emotionally agitated or drained, and in a frame of mind that would allow the teacher to easily drive home a personal point of view. This happens far too often without teachers even realizing it. For example, a teacher who is committed to a particular interpretation of the American role in the Vietnam War ought to offer at least some reference to opposing positions. Showing the film *Hearts and Minds* (1974) in a class on Vietnam would have students at the edge of their seats, ready to understand and accept any arguments presented about why the war was a waste of American youth and a crime against the people of Southeast Asia. But using the film in this way is tantamount to manipulating and propagandizing the students. At the very least, class discussion of such a film should address the ways its powerful images and editing techniques may serve to move viewers unconsciously toward an antiwar position. There are scores of productions that address the United States as a world power, the role of women in society, politics in the Third World, and numerous other issues. Teachers who decide to use them in class owe it to the students to help them understand the ways the films may work on their emotions.

It is also important that history teachers remember the goals of their lessons, without straying too much into the interesting questions concerning film and television or the popular perception of the media today. These subjects would be appropriate at some level, but they may often lead discussion away from the historical issues that should be central to a history class.

Where the equipment is available, one particularly effective way to familiarize students with visual language is to have them produce their own short films or videotapes. Even without production equipment, students often enjoy projects that involve scripting or storyboarding a production without actually filming it, or they might put together a slide-tape presentation of some kind. Such projects should be carefully designed to keep historical questions in focus. Students might be required to outline several alternative narrative structures for a film on a particular historical subject, considering how the narrative structure, the types of visual materials available, or the mix of music and narration chosen for the sound track of each potential film might influence the way it interprets its historical subject. Whenever history students make films or videotapes as class projects, they should be asked to consider their interpretive approach and how the narrative structure and the visual and aural content contribute to, or detract from, that point of view.

A good approach for dealing with television news is to ask students to compare stories covered in newspapers and on TV. They will quickly discover that television news gives them only a tiny percentage of the information they can get from the newspaper, but they should be encouraged to make the comparison on a deeper level. The class should consider the other news of importance during a given day or week. As an activity, the students can do a shot-by-shot breakdown of a particular TV news story and study how the visual context and use of sound may have influenced the perception viewers had of the information presented. It may help to take a few moments to contrast the relatively subtle elements of bias in today's television news with the comparatively bombastic commentaries and musical sound tracks of the newsreel examples provided in the video compilation. Students can then compare the ways different TV news broadcasts and different newspapers covered the same story. By surveying the news of an entire week, students will be able to note trends in the ways different media handle developing situations. For a modest fee to cover their costs, the Vanderbilt Television News Archive will compile thirty minutes of television news stories on any topic from the three networks and lend this tape for use in research or classroom study. An effective lesson might be designed around some event of national importance that took place locally since 1969 (when Vanderbilt started taping), by ordering a compilation of stories about the event as covered on the various networks and comparing that with local newspaper and national news magazine coverage.

The most effective way students can learn from moving images is through discussion. The teacher should try to guide classroom film discussions, without controlling the response of the class too strongly or too obviously. If the self-evident purpose of the film discussion is to draw out only a specific set of responses desired by the teacher, participation by those students who are too afraid or embarrassed to risk a "wrong" answer—one different from that the teacher wanted—might be discouraged. For this reason it is often best to begin the discussion by asking questions that do not require the students to reach independent judgments about the meaning of a film. If the film adds insight to a theme the class has been studying, the students will usually find it for themselves, and particular points that are missed can always be made later.

One especially effective way of encouraging this unpressured participation, which lays the groundwork for productive discussions, is called the sight-sound skim. The object of this method is to begin the discussion of a film by asking the students simply to describe what they saw, that is, to describe the images that were projected on the screen as they come to mind. The teacher might reduce the descriptions to one- or two-word image labels and fill the blackboard with the words that identify the images. If the film has a story line, the teacher might try reconstructing the plot with the parlor-game technique in which student after student retells the story one incident after another. From here the discussion can progress in several different directions, but already the students have been able to participate in a natural and unpressured way, and the sometimes subliminal images from the film have been transformed into conscious, shared ideas for the class to consider.

When considering a more or less didactic educational film such as *The Twenties* (1969), a class discussion might proceed as follows: The teacher would prepare a blackboard list of image labels, including flappers, speakeasies, Calvin Coolidge, the stock market, automobile assembly lines, the Wall Street crash, and several dozen more. Students might be asked to group the words into appropriate categories. What, if anything, have flappers and speakeasies to do with Calvin Coolidge? Should automobile assembly lines and the Wall Street crash be considered as somehow tied together? The teacher might also ask the class to reconstruct the order in which the images were presented and decide if some reordering might alter the historical interpretation suggested by the film. A group of students could be assigned to create its own scenario for a film on the same subject or arrange still photographs in a way that conveys an interpretive message different from the one they have just seen.

Under some circumstances, the teacher might decide to let the class lead itself. Especially when dealing with short experimental films, many of which are plotless, full of animation and cinematic devices, and open to individual interpretation, it may be worthwhile to allow the sight-sound skimming to continue, with the students exploring more deeply their own personal reactions to the film. The short film *Time Piece* (1965) can be used in this way. This film uses animation, trick photography, a playful musical sound track, and some obvious cinematic symbols to comment on life in the urban-suburban rat race of the mid-1960s. The students can discuss the images until an interpretation of the film starts to emerge. Then they might be asked to identify other images that support or refute this interpretation. At first glance, an experimental film like *Time Piece* might seem to have little practical application in the history classroom. Its contrived plot and frenetic style of editing make it totally unsatisfactory for imparting factual information. But when it is used as the basis of a freewheeling class discussion, such an imaginative film can provide an effective exercise in the techniques of visual communication and result in a heightened potential for historical thinking and critical evaluation.

Another valuable approach in teaching with film is to have students consider their own feelings and emotions when discussing how the film influenced them. The teacher might ask the students what they experienced while watching *Triumph of the Will*: What emotions were evoked by particular images—the plane descending from the clouds, or the uniformed men marching into the stadium with shovels on their shoulders in place of guns? How and why might the feelings of Germans in 1935 have differed from the students' own? Which of the images in the film were intended primarily to convey information, to introduce the German people to the new Nazi leaders, for example, and which were meant to engender an emotional response of pride or fear? Perhaps for students today the emotions evoked by the 1964 "Daisy Spot" would have more meaning. Students might be asked to consider what they felt when the screen was engulfed in the nuclear explosion and then discuss whether the emotion was more the creation of a skilled advertising film producer or a reasonable response to the issues at hand.

There are some films so emotionally powerful that they defy frame-by-frame analysis. Alain Resnais's *Night and Fog*, for example, presents a stark view of the Nazi concentration camps and contrasts pictures of the camps in full operation with tranquil scenes of the camps ten years later. The film includes confiscated German movies of Jews helping each other into cattle cars and postwar pictures of the gas chambers with fingernail marks scratched into the concrete ceilings. The feelings of shock and revulsion, especially for students who cannot quite believe that such things really happened, are beyond the scope of a typical class discussion, and a sight-sound skim might even diminish the impact of the experience. What the teacher might do, however, is wait a day or two after showing the film and then have the students discuss the Nuremberg trials; the discussion should give the teacher some idea of the impact the film had on the class. Alternatively, the teacher might ask the students to write about the role of individual moral judgment within society, then view the film, and a day or two later reconsider their own ideas.

There are three basic rules for the teacher using film. First, the teacher should be as well prepared as possible. On the day a teacher brings a film into class, more work may be required than on a typical day. The teacher should always preview a film before showing it to the students. In addition, the teacher should always prepare the class for a film and provide an introduction. One exception to this might be with short, experimental films intended for individual interpretation, in which the teacher's introductory comments might undermine the students' personal involvement with the film. Most films shown in the history classroom, however, have a specific message to convey, and a few preliminary remarks will help the students to observe more carefully. When showing a film for analysis as a document, the teacher should identify it as specifically as possible—a newsreel, a historical documentary, a feature film—and provide background information so students can view the film with some points of reference. Finally, with all this preparation, the teacher must be ready to learn with the students too.

Second, the teacher should use film and video only when it works well as film or video. Some educational films, like televised lectures canned for replay, picture a teacher standing by a blackboard or sitting in an easy chair. These films may be convenient for the classroom teacher and profitable for the producers, but they are definitely not film experiences for the students, and they should, as a rule, be avoided. If the major value of any film is only in its didactic sound track, the teacher should seek some alternate way to present the material. Full use should be made of audiotapes, sound filmstrips, still photographs, and slides when these can make the point as well as film. These forms are usually less expensive, and using and understanding them will help the student to appreciate the real value and meaning of moving images when they are brought into the classroom.

Finally, the teacher should always integrate the film into the text material of the course and use it as a teaching tool, never as a lesson in itself. A film should not be treated as entertainment or as a reward for a good class. The teacher must always be certain that the students think about the film and consider it a formal and important part of the course. There should be some follow-up to a film experience. If teaching with film involves any threat to good education, that danger is represented by the teacher who tries to let the film do the teaching. Film and television in the classroom should serve to bring the teacher and the students closer together in a mutual learning experience; it should not place an impersonal screen between them.

If such lessons are reinforced with other films, more discussions, readings, and other class materials, the students will become more aware of the psychological and emotional elements of the film experience and more appreciative of the creative potential of the filmmaker's art. Particularly, they will become more critical viewers when they are next faced with a commercial for a political candidate, a television news story on a controversial subject, or a docudrama purporting to tell the complete truth about some historical issue. In addition, the experience of reaching judgments independent of the preordained objectives of the teacher's lesson plan, supplemented with the information gained from the observations of their fellow students in class discussions, cannot help but improve the classroom situation for more traditional units of study. Most important, the students will come to understand some of the dynamics of visual communications and have an opportunity to practice the skills of visual literacy so essential to historical reasoning in the electronic age.

VISUAL LANGUAGE
An Introduction for Historians and History Teachers

When using film or television in a history class, teachers often mistakenly assume that students who have grown up with television, sometimes becoming familiar with the kids on Sesame Street before they know the ones who live next door, are particularly sensitive to visual communications. They are not. Recognizing that most students spend the literal equivalent of years before the television screen, teachers should not confuse familiarity with sensitivity or critical understanding.

Another false assumption is that people do not have to be taught to look at pictures, that unlike learning to read, understanding what is seen is a function that comes naturally. On the contrary, the kind of visual skill that people develop more or less automatically over years of familiarity with a medium such as television is an ability to identify its conventions and decode its surface messages. Viewers can (and do) teach themselves to "get the message" that they are intended to get. What they must be taught is how to comprehend more deeply. This skill can provide viewers with the capacity to appreciate more fully the creative artistry of film and television and, on a more important level, teach them to identify bias and avoid erroneous conclusions.

Cliches such as "the camera can't lie" and "a picture is worth a thousand words" are often used to defend the supposed infallibility of visual evidence. Students beginning to study visual language will immediately see the foolishness of such statements. For almost a century filmmakers have been convincing audiences to accept artifice as reality, at least for the time spent in the theater before the screen. Similarly, a picture may be worth tens of thousands of different words to different people because, in comparison with a verbal expression, a picture is so much more open to individual interpretation. As with any verbal set of signs or symbols, the language and idiom of the moving image can be understood on numerous levels. Graduate students in filmmaking or television production must be fluent in that language if they are to learn to be creative in it. Critical viewers may require a different level of visual literacy, but it is no less important that such learning be addressed directly in the history classroom.

This introduction to visual language is meant to serve as a general and selective guide for history teachers new to the critical use of moving-image media in the classroom. It is keyed to two comprehensive volumes on the subject, which are recommended for further study: James Monaco's *How To Read a Film*, rev. ed. (New York, 1981) and David Bordwell and Kristin Thompson's *Film Art: An Introduction*, 2d ed. (New York, 1986). Although these books may provide more information than the average history teacher needs to know, each is a valuable resource to have on hand to answer questions that may arise while "reading" visual documents in the classroom. In combination with further reading, the following summary should assist teachers in training their students for visual literacy, so that the use of audiovisual materials in the history classroom will take on new importance. In addition to offering interesting information and motivating further study of historical questions, informed moving-image lessons will help develop in students a new set of skills necessary for full participation in today's visual civilization.

The Historical Development of the Moving Image

One convenient way for the history teacher to encourage students to think about the differences between verbal and visual communications is to trace the events leading to the invention of moving-image technology. In this context, there were three historical preconditions that had to be met before the Lumière brothers could set up their first public exhibition of moving pictures.

First, there had to be a recognition of the physiological response that makes movies "work" for people. It is worth making the point with students that moving pictures really do not move. What appears on the screen is a succession of still images, a phenomenon that was applied in parlor toys such as the zoetrope as early as the 1830s (see the illustration in Monaco, 55; Bordwell and Thompson, 3). The traditional explanation—the persistence of vision—holds that the retina of the human eye retains an image for a fraction of a second before it is replaced by another image. Current authorities prefer other explanations based in perceptual psychology (see Bordwell and Thompson, 16-17), but all agree that human perception of the moving-image media is a trick that the eyes play on the mind. Noting this in class will help students to realize the vast potential for psychological influence and interpretation of the moving images they see.

The second precondition for the invention of the movies was the development of photography. The zoetrope device used stick figures or drawn images, because in 1834, when the zoetrope was patented, the invention of photography was still five years in the future. Teachers should present the historical evolution of photography, from the camera obscura of Leonardo da Vinci's time to the early photographic processes of the 1840s and 1850s, which for the first time allowed the permanent recording and reproduction of an image. Subsequently, photographic technology had to be improved and exposure speed increased to allow photographing of eighteen to twenty-four frames per second, the minimum necessary for the succession of images to convey the appearance of motion. By the mid-1880s exposure speeds had shortened to the point where John Muybridge could experiment with flanks of cameras that could stop the action of a galloping horse, in an effort to establish whether all four hooves left the ground at the same time.

The third precondition for movies, at least silent movies, was the invention of the moving-picture camera, which allowed a series of pictures each second to be exposed through the same lens, and the moving-picture projector. By the mid-1880s George Eastman had developed and marketed a flexible film to replace the glass plates in use by photographers. In 1889 Thomas Edison and his colleagues developed the first practical moving-picture camera, which could manipulate the flexible film so that it could be brought to a complete stop before the aperture, exposed, and moved on again at least eighteen times per second. For the next decade Edison devoted considerable money and effort to the marketing of the kinetoscope, a peephole viewing device that was set up in public viewing parlors (see Monaco, 58-59).

The development of equipment to project a moving image was left to two Frenchmen. The challenge to project eighteen to twenty-four discrete images successively within one second, including a fraction of a second of black screen between each image (without the screen going black between each frame, viewers would see a blur instead of the illusion of smooth, even motion), was met by the Lumière brothers, who first publicly presented projected moving pictures in Paris in 1895.

Although new technological developments in recorded sound, color photography, and the entirely new medium of television would alter the way people looked at film, the basic elements of the moving-image media were in place by 1895.

Functional Components of Moving-Image Media

The basic element of a film is the shot. Although it might vary in duration from a fraction of a second to several minutes, a shot is defined as a single, unedited, continuously exposed piece of film. One or more shots that detail a single action at a single location make up a scene. One or more scenes that constitute a natural unit of narration are referred to as a sequence. Thus, there might be a sequence that begins with a scene on a railroad track where a man catches his foot. That scene might be several shots long, as the camera offers an establishing shot of the location, a medium shot of the man walking, and a close-up of his foot as it slips into a crevice next to the track, followed by another close-up of the look of fright on his face as he hears the whistle of a train approaching from around the bend. At this point, the film might cut to another scene inside the locomotive, where the engineer casually lights his pipe and checks his gauges. Subsequent scenes would be made up of other combinations of shots and strung together on a unifying theme to complete the sequence.

Many film scholars would say that it is too limiting to the film medium to suggest the following comparison, but beginning students may find it helpful to compare the parts of a film to the parts of a book:

shot = sentence
scene = paragraph
sequence = chapter
film = book

In the same way that a sentence, rather than a word, is the basic constituent element of verbal language (unless it is a one-word sentence expressing a complete idea), so the shot, rather than the individual frame, is the basic unit of film. The various elements within a shot and the editing devices through which shots, scenes, and sequences are linked together are what give the moving-image media their creative capacity to mold time and space for dramatic effect. The two essential visual components of moving-image communication are therefore the elements of the individual shot and the editing devices through which shots are given meaning in relation to one another. The meaning of individual shots and edited scenes and sequences is also influenced by the sound track, and sound therefore contributes as much information as the images it accompanies.

Elements of a shot. When authors write sentences, they have certain creative tools at their command. They can choose from a dictionary full of words, combine words in various ways, and use punctuation to accent their meaning. They can organize phrases within sentences to modify one another, limiting or accentuating ideas or adding nuances of meaning. Filmmakers have at least as much creative latitude.

The elements of a motion-picture shot are of two general types. First, there is mise-en-scène, the things literally put in the shot to create its narrative content. Mise-en-scène includes aspects of staging, creative design, and dramatic direction that would be present whether a production were being prepared for the stage or for the movie screen. Elements of mise-en-scène in a historic dramatization, for example, would include the setting (whether a scene was shot on a studio set or on location), the props and costumes that identify the scene with the appropriate historical period, the casting of characters, and the elements of dramatic expression that actors bring to their parts.

It is possible for mise-en-scène to be handled with particular sensitivity in a historical film, especially when filmmakers rely on the expertise of professional historians as consultants, such as Natalie Zemon Davis in the production of *The Return of Martin Guerre*. In the video compilation Davis comments on the care that went into documentation of mise-en-scène, including the color of the wedding dress, the words of the marriage vows, and the nature of the dowry offerings, though some details were still overlooked. Mise-en-scène can also contribute to historical interpretation. The scene in which a notary draws up the marriage contract while the newlywed couple sits quietly by, includes many ordinary daily activities (tending the fire, making the bread, plucking a chicken), which reinforce the point that matters of marriage and the extended family were central concerns in the everyday life of the time. On the other hand, it was not historically correct to include a large gathering of townspeople in the back of the room in the final court scenes of the film, but the filmmakers wanted to show reactions to the testimony being given and to emphasize how the issue of Martin Guerre's identity had come to concern the entire community. *The Return of Martin Guerre* was given a heightened aura of authenticity through recently developed light-sensitive camera lenses and film stock, which allowed photographing of the interior of sixteenth-century houses with light levels roughly as they must have been, thereby avoiding the use of obtrusive artificial lighting.

More commonly, a film is considered historically accurate in terms of mise-en-scène as long as there are no glaring incongruities or anachronisms—no eyeglasses on Julius Caesar or jet trails in a cloudless eighteenth-century sky. Obviously, the theatrical filmmaker can have more influence over mise-en-scène than can the documentarist, who does not costume the people being interviewed or direct them in delivering their lines for dramatic effect. When coproducers Suzanne Bauman and Rita Heller took their cameras to a reunion of participants in the Bryn Mawr summer program for women, interviewees were given no scripted lines to read. Like all other filmmakers, however, Bauman and Heller retained ultimate control, deciding whether to include any or all of an interview in the completed film and arranging the interview segments in an order (intercut with stills and archival footage) that supported the message that *Women of Summer* was intended to convey (see the video compilation).

The photographic elements of a shot make up the second general category, and they are as important in working with documentaries as they are with theatrical films. Because images are observed "naturally," and because so many people have had the experience of taking their own casual snapshot pictures of family and friends, viewers may assume that the photographic images presented in moving-image media simply happened that way. Most filmmakers strive for the look of naturalness, but the skillful filmmaker maintains intimate control over all visual elements, continually working to assure that each contributes to conveying both the information and the feeling that is to be projected. Just as no sentence in a serious work of literature can be thought of as an unplanned jumble of words, no shot in a creditable film simply "happens" before the camera.

Some of the major creative elements that the filmmaker or television producer uses to make each shot communicate specific ideas and emotions include duration, lighting, color, field size, composition, camera angle, camera movement, focus, lens characteristics, film stock, and projection speed. (With the exception of duration, camera movement, and projection speed, each of these elements relates as well to the still photograph.)

- **Duration.** The length in time that a shot is on the screen varies from a fraction of a second to several minutes and can influence a shot's meaning significantly. Depending on the complexity of the shot, a certain time will be necessary for the viewer to absorb the information. Generally, the eye needs more time to read a wide-angle establishing shot than it does a close-up. The viewer's attention may be directed from one part of the image to another by changing compositional elements and camera movements. An image that stays on the screen longer than is necessary for its information to be conveyed invites the viewer to ponder its meaning more deeply, to good or bad effect. (See Bordwell and Thompson, 187-91, 205-207.)

- **Lighting.** The direction and intensity of lighting and the use of shadow can have an overpowering impact on the meaning of an image. Dark shadows can convey an air of mystery. By showing huge combines harvesting at night (Figure E) as part of the "Twenties Boom" sequence of *The Plow*, Pare Lorentz was able to indicate a passion for productivity. By showing them lit starkly from behind, he was able to add a note of ominous foreboding (further accented by the music). Facial features can be altered dramatically by lighting, as many an aging actor can attest. (See Monaco, 158-59, 166-69; Bordwell and Thompson, 126-31.) Bordwell and Thompson include lighting as an element of mise-en-scène, and, indeed, it is one of the elements of stage and set design most important in both live theater and theatrical film, but it should be recognized as a photographic element as well.

- **Color.** Both hue and intensity of color are important for their overall emotional influence and for specific color symbolism. Lighting, film stock, and lens filters offer varied creative possibilites. (See Monaco, 96-98, 156-57; Bordwell and Thompson, 130-31, 136-37, 152-53, 192 -93.)

- **Field Size.** The distance of the action from the camera affects viewers' relationship with what they see. The field size may result in a long shot, a medium shot, a close-up, or a limitless variety of shot distances in between these general parameters. Typically, a long shot, especially when used as an establishing shot, conveys context by establishing the orientation between setting and characters, while a close-up (of a facial expression, for example) has more potential for dramatic interpretation. The image of an overflowing grain hopper (Figure F) in *The Plow* accentuates the volume of production because the sides of the bin are not shown. (See Monaco, 161; Bordwell and Thompson, 169-74.)

- **Composition.** The way a shot is composed affects the balance of the image and guides the viewer's eye to the most important elements. Images may be composed sparely or loaded with detail. They may be closed (strictly limited to the boundaries of the frame) or open (implicitly or explicitly referring to characters and spaces outside the camera's view). There are also recognized conventions of composition, such as the establishing shot and the reverse-angle shot, and important symbolic codes regarding gesture and body language. (See Monaco, 140-60; Bordwell and Thompson, 136-37, 162-87.)

- **Camera Angle.** High angle, low angle, dutch angle, and the many angle variations in between influence attitude toward the action and the subjects. If a woman is shot from a low angle, she seems dominant and powerful. The opposite is usually true of high-angle shots, which put the viewer on a higher or superior plane. A tilted, or dutch, angle might suggest disorientation of either the subject, the viewer, or both. The extreme low-angle shot near the opening of *The Plow*, which highlights individual blades of grass against the sky (Figure G), can be read as emphasizing their vulnerability. Later in the film, the low-angle shot of a farm buried in wind-blown dust (Figure H) makes the situation appear much worse than would a shot photographed from an elevated platform. (See Monaco, 164, 172; Bordwell and Thompson, 168ff.)

- **Camera Movement.** Each movement of the camera serves to extend and change the frame and the composition in ways that can advance the narrative thread of a film or offer interpretive comments. The camera can pan, track, dolly, tilt, or crane, as well as vary in speed of movement. (See Monaco, 77-80; Bordwell and Thompson, 174-87.)

- **Focus.** There are many ways focus can be used within a shot. Focus can direct viewers' attention within the frame, and it can be altered within the context of the shot to redirect that attention elsewhere. Sharp focus may convey a realistic, sometimes harsh impression; soft focus may convey a dreamy, romantic feeling. (See Monaco, 162-64; Bordwell and Thompson, 156-59.)

- **Lens Characteristics.** Various lenses—telephoto and wide-angle are the most common—and the characteristics specific to them can

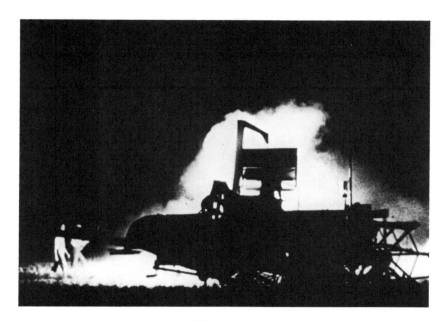

Figure E

Figure F

Figure G

Figure H

alter the scope and relative size of the image photographed. Lenses also affect the speed of action to and from the camera. A telephoto lens slows the action and a wide-angle lens speeds it up. Depth of field will also affect the image; more depth is in focus in a wide-angle shot and less in a telephoto. A zoom lens allows shifting from one set of characteristics to another within the same shot, but its effects should not be confused with camera movements like dollying in or out from the scene. (See Monaco, 60-64; Bordwell and Thompson, 156-61.)

- **Film Stock.** Qualities of the film stock play an important role in the qualities of the image produced. Characteristics of film emulsion, speed of exposure, and differences in the processing of film in the laboratory contribute to such visual qualities as graininess and color quality. The differences are comparable to the effects achieved by a portrait photographer, who uses slow film, as opposed to a newspaper photographer, who characteristically works with very fast film to increase contrast and stop action. (See Monaco, 81-82, 159; Bordwell and Thompson, 151-54.)

- **Projection Speed.** While most film is recorded and projected at the same speed, action can be artificially slowed or accelerated by altering either the speed of the camera or the projector. This can also be accomplished in the laboratory by repeating individual frames in such a way as to extend and slow action. (See Bordwell and Thompson, 155-56.)

The experience of watching any moving-image presentation on film or video inevitably involves the viewer in decoding these various elements. To a large extent, that decoding goes on unconsciously, as viewers respond to the cues they have been informally taught to respond to through years of movie and television watching. Viewers usually see what filmmakers intend them to see, and they "get the message" they are supposed to get.

The idea of visual literacy, especially when understood in the context of history and social studies, involves being able to see beyond (or through) what the filmmakers intended, to become aware of the ways creative elements may have been used by the filmmaker to produce the desired impression on the audience and then reasonably evaluate whether that point of view is supported by facts and evidence. In the same way that people learn to critically identify words or phrases that are loaded or colored with bias and may influence their overall perception of an article or a book, visually literate people should also be conscious of the ways in which individual images and combinations of images can be loaded or colored.

Editing: Joining image to image. In addition to understanding the elements of the individual shot, the visually literate person must have an appreciation of the importance of editing for creative communication in the moving-image media. On a simple level, editing devices can be thought of as punctuation marks, which may give hints, though not always reliable indications, of the relationship that is intended. There are a limited number of ways that shots or sequences can be joined together:

- **Fade.** The introduction (fade in) or removal (fade out) of the image onto a blank screen usually indicates either the beginning or end of some dramatic action, or some passage of time.

- **Dissolve.** The gradual overlapping of images in which one comes to replace another usually suggests a relationship between the two shots. Like a fade, a dissolve can happen quickly or be drawn out over several seconds.

- **Wipe.** The mechanical moving of one image off the screen and the replacing of it with another is called a wipe. Examples of wipes include directional replacement of images (such as from right to left), replacement from the center of the screen with an iris, or box replacement from a corner of the screen, which expands until the screen is completely filled with the new image. The wipe is an old-fashioned device more common in silent film than in recent cinema, but it is used today in television, especially for special effects in sports programming. It is generally used to break continuity and mark the beginning of or radical shift to some new action.

- **Cut.** The instantaneous replacing of one image with another is at once the most common editing device and the one most open to interpretation. The cut can, for example, be used in a shot/reverse shot sequence to reinforce the continuity of action happening at the same time and place; in a cross-cutting situation (relating images of a maiden in distress, for example, with those of the hero rushing to her rescue), in which action may be happening at the same time but in different places; or, at the extreme, in a jump cut that leaps across continents of space or centuries of time.

Since history is to a very considerable extent concerned with matters of place and time, editing is of special significance, for it is in joining images one to another that moving-image media's ability to creatively represent (or misrepresent) space and time is most evident. Within the individual shot, for example, there are ways that time can seemingly be expanded or compressed: through under- or overcranking of the camera, through use of lenses that appear to slow or speed action to or from the camera, through laboratory processes such as the use of the optical printer. There are also ways place can seemingly be altered, such as through camera movement or changes in focus, but none of these has the potential for altering place and time that the editing together of images has.

In the 1920s the Russian filmmaker and theorist Lev Kuhlesov experimented with the ways audiences understood images presented one after another, without the help of an establishing shot to give viewers their bearings. When he reproduced the same image of a face (that of a famous Russian actor) several times, and presented it in conjunction with an image of a bowl of soup, a baby, and a dead woman laid out in a coffin, viewers praised the subtlety of the actor in expressing hunger in relation to the soup, love in relation to the baby, and grief in relation to the corpse. Though the images of the actor's face were exactly the same, people saw what they expected to see. In the absence of evidence to the contrary, such as establishing shots that might have indicated that the images were not related to one another, viewers assumed that the shots paired on the screen took place at the same place and time and, going one step further, presumed that the images were related to one another causally. (See Monaco, 323; Bordwell and Thompson, 160-61.)

The Kuhlesov effect is usually thought of in relation to individual pairs of images, but the impetus of an audience to associate shots to one another, and to see what they are led to believe they are seeing, goes much farther. Almost all historical compilation films (those compiled from various pieces of archival footage on some historical issue or event) are forced to rely on some amount of stock footage to fill in gaps in the extant actuality materials. A shot of planes flying overhead may cut to an anti-aircraft gun shooting into the sky, and then to a plane in flames hurtling toward the earth. The likelihood that a camera operator was in the perfect position to record these three shots of the shooting down of an individual plane is slim. It is much more likely that the sequence was constructed from three separate shots taken at different locations at different times, and edited together to provide the desired effect in the mind of the viewer. This does not necessarily destroy the information content of the film. Planes may actually have been shot down. But the editing of the scene should provide a warning that the truthfulness of the message of a film may have relatively little connection with the specific images that appear on the screen.

What members of an audience thought they saw, or were tricked into thinking they saw, may be of special interest historically. Nicholas Pronay of the University of Leeds studied British newsreels of the early days of World War II, which were carefully constructed (with the encouragement of the British government) to reassure the English people as they suffered through the dark days of the blitz. One newsreel story that especially interested Pronay extolled the abilities of British anti-

64

aircraft units and their weapons. The newsreel included a long shot of a gun firing at a range far beyond that which British weapons could reach. By studying the image closely, Pronay established what audiences of the time could not have noticed from the screen: the film was actually of a German gun. Pronay's work is instructive not only for the ways he demonstrates how footage was falsified in newsreel film, but also for the propagandistic effect it reveals. In this case, it is more important for the historian to understand what people thought they saw than what they actually did see.

Perhaps the ultimate example of such falsification in a historical film involves "Victory at Sea" (1952), one of the first great television compilation series. When interviewed by historian Peter C. Rollins, series producer Isaac Klienerman claimed to be most proud of the program on the Battle of Leyte Gulf, still used in the 1970s for strategic study at the Naval War College. Making this film presented a particular challenge, because there were no cameras at Leyte Gulf. The producers made up the film completely of stock footage and film shot of other battles. Such wholesale falsification certainly raises questions about the reliability of compilation films, but the historical information and interpretation presented in a film depends on more than the veracity of the archival footage. There may indeed be very valuable historical observations in the Battle of Leyte Gulf program that have nothing to do with where the pictures of the ships came from. This film is more important as it illustrates the importance of critical viewing. Viewers must be able to comprehend and evaluate the messages of a presentation based on real evidence. They should not allow themselves to simply be swept along by a film on the false premise that, through the film, they are on the scene themselves, reliving the experience of the time, and therefore capable of making their own judgments about it.

In contrast to the production methods employed in the Battle of Leyte Gulf program, most makers of historical compilation films today, especially those trained as historical scholars who have in addition become filmmakers, make it a cardinal rule to use only footage that can be verified as being from the same time and place (or at least from the same general period) as the subject they are working on. This does not mean that most errors in historical films are due to the falsification of footage. On the contrary, most of the potential for problems, like most of the potential for success, lies in the ways the filmmakers choose the footage, and how that footage is edited into a final product. Viewers must be aware that even guarantees that a film was made solely from archival footage of the time and place in question in no way assures that the film presents a complete or truthful account.

The newsreel archives in which producers of historical compilation films conduct much of their research are rich with examples of how footage was selected and edited for the presentation of news stories. The outtakes are sometimes more valuable to historians than the footage the newsreel companies put on the screen. The video compilation includes several examples of the ways newsreel film was selected and edited for release, including footage of President Franklin D. Roosevelt not used in the newsreel because it showed him in a position that made obvious his physical infirmity, and a story on the Berlin airlift that demonstrates the extent to which events were often staged for the newsreel cameras.

Like newsreels, television news offers important nightly examples of the creative use of editing in the presentation of actuality footage. Time constraints and the capsulized nature of most television news stories make it likely that fuller coverage can almost always be found in the printed media, but the concept of the viewer as an eyewitness is a powerful one. It suggests that viewers relate to news on television at least in part with the rationalization that they are better able to see and evaluate a situation for themselves than they might be when reading a newspaper story. To counteract this assumption, students should be helped to understand how editing can influence viewers subconsciously. On one level, the ordering of stories in a broadcast, and their organization in relation to commercials, suggests their relative importance. On another level, as it should be clear to visually literate viewers, the editing of each story, from thirty seconds to four minutes of video that might include several interviews, voice-over comments on otherwise silent footage, and on-camera commentary by the anchor person, is crucial to the message the story conveys. On the most basic level, critical viewers must learn about the construction of the typical television interview.

A basic TV news crew includes a reporter, a camera operator, and a sound person. When the crew goes on location to interview someone, their first concern is to photograph the person speaking words that they can later use in an edited story. Typically, they will set up the camera for an establishing shot of the interviewee and the reporter, and then concentrate the camera on recording the person's responses to the reporter's questions. After they have the material they need—often after the interviewee has left the scene—they will set up the camera again in reverse angle to photograph the reporter, who repeats the questions once more. Since it is rare for more than one camera to be sent out with a news crew, this process is necessary to give the editor raw material to work with when constructing the final piece for broadcast. Presumably, the reporter repeats the questions in exactly the same words, using exactly the same inflection as the first time, but it is easy to imagine how, having already heard what the subject is going to say, there might be some changes. At this point, the reporter may also do a few silent reaction shots, trying to appear as though listening to the interviewee's response, and a stand-up introduction to the story with some identifiable landmark in the background.

When the news crew returns to the station with the raw footage, the work is only half finished. The various pieces photographed in the field then have to be arranged in such a way that they present the story as clearly and concisely as possible, in accordance with the time constraints of the broadcast. Viewers frequently assume that the various elements of a completed story took place in the order in which they were presented, not stopping to think that the editor of a televised news story frequently writes the introduction last. Most viewers are also unaware that the actual order of interview comments or other recorded elements may have been rearranged in a number of different ways.

One selection in the video compilation illustrates how such interviews are created, showing how comments from an extended conversation, recorded with a single camera, can be reduced, rearranged, and reoriented through editing with cutaways. The interview begins with a two-shot (a shot showing two persons, in this case an establishing shot), in which the person being interviewed is photographed from behind the shoulder of the interviewer. In the same shot, the lens zooms in so that the interviewee is speaking directly into the camera. The second shot is a cutaway, or reaction shot, of the interviewer listening attentively to the interviewee, who is still heard speaking on the sound track. In the third shot, the camera is shifted back to the interviewee. In the first and third shots, the sound is synchronized with the image, but in the second, where the sound synch is lost, it becomes possible to delete or rearrange words, sentences, or entire paragraphs of what the interviewee is saying. If there is even an approximate match in the tone and cadence of the voice and the logic of what is being said, viewers (and listeners) would not be likely to notice the audio cuts.

There might be several editing shifts even in a one- or two-minute interview. In a more lengthy exchange, additional cutaways might be used for visual variety. One of the most interesting sequences in Edward R. Murrow's "See It Now: Report on Senator McCarthy" shows McCarthy speaking at a Washington's Birthday celebration in Philadelphia in 1954. Viewers questioned after watching this sequence (included in the video compilation) think that they have just watched two-and-one-half minutes of McCarthy making a speech; they presume that what they have seen on the screen took place just as they saw it, in real time. A closer viewing reveals that the sequence was made up of nine shots edited together to allow a compression of McCarthy's forty-minute speech into a tight and coherent statement for the program. The sequence contains three cutaways, one to the upper part of the mural in front of which McCarthy spoke and two to the audience. Each provided an opportunity for the editors to trim McCarthy's comments down to what they could use. Without the outtakes from the editing session or a transcript of McCarthy's entire speech, viewers cannot know how much was deleted. They can be quite sure, however, that the attentive audience members shown in the cutaways were not being attentive to McCarthy saying what is heard on the second track. CBS had only one camera present at the event, and it would not have been focused anywhere but on the platform while the senator was speaking. The audience shots would have been photographed either before or after McCarthy spoke so that the editors would have material to vary the news report.

The cutaway is an essential tool for television news and documentary producers, who must almost always cut down a longer interview to fit a short time slot. The editors can delete much from a person's responses, even combining the answers to several questions into one, by simply making the audio cuts coincide with a visual cutaway. Another option is to delete material while cutting to a shot of the reporter asking (actually repeating) a different question. The viewers unsuspectingly assume that the interview is taking place in real time and that the sequence of questions and answers is a seamless record of what happened. In any television interview, but especially in footage that includes repeated cuts back and forth from the reporter to the subject, viewers should be aware that every reaction shot and every cut to the interviewer with a new question provides an occasion for a reduction or rearrangement of the audio.

It should be stressed that rather than meaning to misrepresent what is said, TV news editors usually intend only to avoid distracting visual choppiness in the finished product. Although the subjects of TV interviews may come across better in edited form, sometimes they react negatively to being edited. Perhaps the most famous controversy over cutaways involved CBS News and its 1970 documentary "The Selling of the Pentagon." Claiming that cutaways were used not only to condense, but also to rearrange and garble responses made by Pentagon spokesmen, the government forced the issue until hearings were held before a congressional committee on the practice of television news editing.

To teach students about such basic processes in the production of television news is not to call for different standards in TV news editing. The problem lies less with the producers and editors (people performing their craft the best way they know) than with viewers who may prefer to watch TV news because it seems like so much less work than reading the newspaper. Students must be brought to understand that critical viewing of a moving image, especially an important one such as a news story on a significant public issue, should demand at least as much attention as the careful reading of a printed page.

The main concern of the theatrical or documentary filmmaker in making decisions about editing is similar to the concern of the TV news editor. The filmmaker's goal is to create film sequences in which viewers are encouraged to concentrate on the point being made without being unnecessarily distracted by confusing shifts in subject, camera location, camera angle, or composition. Continuity editing is the procedure of joining together pieces of film in ways that prevent such disorientation.

Camera angle, for example, is important in retaining continuity. If a woman is seen leaving a room in one direction, it is important that the shot showing her entering the adjoining room be at an angle that does not disorient the viewer. An audience would certainly find it hard to follow a chase scene in which the train robbers were portrayed riding from the left to the right side of the screen intercut with a posse trailing them from right to left. There are various ways shots can be joined together to emphasize a sense of continuity, such as the seamless continuation of some motion or sound element from one shot to the next, or the composition of the second shot so that the focal point of interest is in the same location on the screen that it was in the preceding shot.

Over the years, a series of editing conventions developed that influenced the ways in which viewers interpreted what was going on in the narrative of a film story. The editing conventions of the classical Hollywood cinema of the thirties and forties, for example, dictated that a scene between two characters begin with an establishing shot and then progress through a series of shot/reverse shots showing close-ups of each character speaking to the other. The selection in the video compilation that includes two alternate editing patterns for the climactic sequence from *The Life of an American Fireman* (1902) demonstrates how audiences at the turn of the century had different expectations when they tried to make sense of a filmed story. Perhaps because of their experience with live theater, the audiences for early motion pictures were more comfortable with editing patterns that preserved the continuity of space, preferring to see all the action from one point of view at a time, even if that action had to be repeated from the start to show them another point of view. In contrast, classical Hollywood cinema style was based on a continuity of time in which editing shifted freely from one point of view to another, but never showed the same event twice. The version of *The Life of an American Fireman* that was subsequently re-edited according to the more modern style illustrates the power of editing in leading viewers through a narrative. Careful viewing of the original version reveals a number of incongruities (people entering the room from the wrong side and windows broken in rather than out, for example), which are difficult to recognize when the logic of the more modern editing style leads the viewer through the scene. Editing conventions do change over time, and they are not always used in the expected ways. Indeed, art may be said to disappear when, through rigorous adherence, convention becomes cliche. (For more on continuity editing and the classical Hollywood cinema, see Bordwell and Thompson, 211-20.)

There are alternatives to continuity editing. Some of the highlights of film history are centered around the creative use of editing to break continuity and interpret reality in artistic ways. An important example is Sergei Eisenstein's use of editing to create a collision of images to visually convey what he saw as the essence of the class struggle, a point he thought would have been much more difficult to convey in a seamless narrative continuity. Other examples include the juxtaposition of individual images in an otherwise traditionally edited film. In *Hearts and Minds* (1974), a documentary tour de force against American involvement in Vietnam, Peter Davis sacrifices continuity for dramatic contrast when he cuts directly from an interview with General William Westmoreland, who is explaining that Oriental people have little respect for life, to a Vietnamese woman weeping openly over the grave of a loved one killed in battle.

Editing is also used to integrate dramatic symbolism into a scene. In the opening shot of Charlie Chaplin's *Modern Times* (1936), a midshot of sheep (including one black sheep) being herded, presumably to the slaughter house, cuts directly to a shot of workers pouring out of a subway exit on their way to work. The rest of the film deals with the ways in which industrial civilization threatens to dehumanize the lives of ordinary people, providing Chaplin's tramp character (a black sheep) with numerous dramatic situations, both humorous and pathetic.

Sound and image. A motion picture or television program engages the ears as well as the eyes. Edison experimented with movies with synchronized sound as early as 1912, and until sound technology was fully implemented in the late 1920s, films were almost always shown with some musical accompaniment (ranging from a concert orchestra to a phonograph record) and even with live sound effects. Once sound technology was in place in theaters, silent films all but disappeared.

Tony Schwartz, the producer of hundreds of successful radio and television commercials, argues that the sound element of a film is almost always more important than the visual. He encourages exercises in which students watch films without the sound and try to work out the meaning before watching them again with the sound. Chris Marker's *Letters From Siberia* (1957) invites viewers to think about the influence of sound by showing the same visual footage three separate times with three different, widely contrasting sound tracks. (See Bordwell and Thompson, 232-33.)

Sound can be diegetic (emanating from a character or object that is part of the story space of the film) or nondiegetic; it can come from on or off screen; it can be internal (relating only to what is going on in the mind of one character) or external; it can be synchronized or asynchronous; and it can extend from shot to shot as a bridge between scenes. The three general types of sound are: the spoken word (dialogue or narration), music, and sound effects. (See Monaco, 178-83; Bordwell and Thompson, 232-57.) The selection in the video compilation from *Women of Summer* provides an especially good opportunity to study all of these various uses of sound.

Sound can contribute significantly to the illusion of realism created in a film. It not only reinforces the believability of what is seen on the screen, but allows the filmmakers to use the area beyond the frame more creatively, for example, with the sound of an approaching locomotive that is heard but not seen. Synchronized sound gives the greatest reinforcement to realism, especially when the sound of voices is lip-synched to the faces doing the speaking. People look natural when speaking on film, but such synchronized sound is very difficult to attain. When a film is projected, the light cell on the projector that picks up the optical sound track comes later in the film path than the lens that projects the image; therefore, the recorded sound on the film must be placed twenty-six frames before the image it accompanies. Although synchronized sound may seem natural to the audience, the filmmakers had to manipulate the materials very unnaturally in order to make it sound that way. (In videotape, the same recording and playback heads handle the audio and video tracks, making the editing of synchronized video considerably more simple.)

When live sound is recorded for film, usually on a tape recorder cabled to the camera, it is crucial that the same speed in the image and the sound track be maintained. Depending on the movement taking place in the frame, the image can be accelerated by as much as 20 percent before the viewers will think the movement unnatural, but the slightest change in the pace of the sound track will alter the pitch of a person's voice and make sound effects seem unreal. Part of the creative flexibility enjoyed by the silent filmmaker was the ability to vary the speed of the camera or the projector for dramatic or humorous effect. Students should be informed, however, that when they see a silent film today in which people seem to be moving about and talking at a faster than normal speed, it is not because the figures were hyperactive or because the filmmakers necessarily intended a Keystone Kops effect. On the contrary, the students are probably watching the film projected at one-and-one-half times the speed that was originally intended. In the early days of moving pictures, film was ordinarily shot and projected at sixteen frames per second. Today, unless step-printed to compensate for the change, early films are often projected at the modern standard of twenty-four frames per second, which results in the unnatural (and unintended) accelerated movement.

Ironically, there are occasions when sound that did happen naturally would seem unreal and confusing in a film. For example, in a war movie in which shells are fired at planes in the distance, the camera cuts quickly from image to image, conveying the excitement of the moment with the pace of the editing. In reality, the sound of the explosion taking place at an altitude of one thousand feet, a half-mile from the camera, would be heard several seconds after the flash was seen. The filmmakers, however, would likely have the sound coincide with the flashes on the screen, so as not to confuse the audience with sounds of explosions accompanying unrelated images.

The use of music on the sound track for a film can be atmospheric, simply setting a tone for the action or the relationships being developed, or it can be a central unifying core of the film's contents. The Nazi propaganda film *Für Uns* (1937) demonstrates this point powerfully, especially if viewers understand the meaning that the musical selections had for Germans in the 1930s. In the opening scenes of the film, as the sixteen martyrs of 1923 are honored as party heroes, the music is the party anthem, "The Horst Wessel Song," played as a mournful durge. Later in the film, when the purpose is to transform these party heroes into national heroes, the party song is replaced with the national anthem. At the close of the film, the music reverts back to "The Horst Wessel Song," played triumphantly in recognition of the Nazis' place as the leaders of the German nation.

Making Meaning from Film and Television

Through the creative combination of mise-en-scène and photographic elements of shots with editing and sound, motion pictures and television communicate meaning in a variety of ways. Because the perception of a moving image requires a level of subconscious psychological involvement, an individual's personality, catalog of previous experiences, and frame of mind are extremely influential on the ways images will be interpreted. Even recognizable symbols convey complex levels of denotative and connotative meaning driven by a variety of physiological, psychological, and cultural factors. Some of these factors are unique to film, while others are drawn from literature and other arts. For example, students unfamiliar with the musical selections in *Für Uns* might simply think of the music as atmospheric background accompaniment and miss the central symbolic role it played in constructing the Nazis' propaganda message.

In film and television, form and content are inseparable. The form and structure of a moving-image production can significantly affect the message presented. Like a painting, a piece of sculpture, or an architect's design for a house, every film has an artistic form, an arrangement of elements intended to interest and involve viewers. In addition to visual and aural elements, there are narrative elements, bits of information about the plot or the characters of a film that lead, maintain, and direct viewers' interest. Not all films are narrative in their formal organization. *The Plow*, for example, like *Für Uns* and the "Daisy Spot," is rhetorical in its structure, intended more to convert its viewers to a point of view than to involve them in a story. (See Bordwell and Thompson, 44-80.)

The range and depth of story information a film reveals, the functions of characters and other plot elements, and the ways the presentation of time is structured (using flashbacks, for example, to fill out a plot) are often the deciding factors when viewers make meaning from a film. They may be allowed an omniscient point of view, seeing many different types of events as they interact with one another, or events may be presented only from the point of view of one of the characters, restricting the information conveyed and building suspense. Viewer expectations are influenced by the film's genre; people watch a mystery film differently than they do a musical. Patterns of development—how the situation at the end of the film differs from the situation at the beginning (has some journey or investigation been completed, has the boy married the girl, has a lesson been learned)—also affect viewer expectations. (See Bordwell and Thompson, 82-112).

By the end of "Molders of Troy," for example, the film has shown how conditions in the iron-molding trade in upstate New York after the Civil War moved the workers to organize and strike. It has also shown how the factory owners responded to the workers with violence and with the decision to move the factories to other cities. The final scene (included in the video compilation) takes place in a tavern, where Jim Donovan, a former worker and union organizer who left the mills to become a city alderman, confronts Brian Duffy, his stepson who is unemployed after being blacklisted as a union agitator. Fearful that Duffy will be hurt if he stays in Troy, Donovan tries to convince him to move to another city, but Duffy resists in the name of principle. The tension between the two characters, and the examination of the issues at hand, is all the more evident to viewers because they have been privileged with information that Donovan does not have. Immediately before Donovan entered the room, Duffy had explained to the bartender that he was already thinking of moving to another town to continue his organizing activities there. Duffy's resistance is a front, a face he puts on for his stepfather, a working man who has succombed to the establishment. It is not the acting style, the editing, or even the scripted lines themselves that allow the audience to make meaning from this scene. It is the narrative structure, in which the line about Duffy's plans to move is inserted immediately before Donovan sits down with him. A structure that withheld this information until after the confrontation, or raised it much earlier in the film, would have radically altered the meaning.

Form is inseparable from content in the narrative strategy of *The Return of Martin Guerre*, the mixing of visual and aural elements in *Women of Summer*, and the editing techniques in *The Life of an American Fireman*. Perhaps the most interesting example of innovative cinema form in the video compilation is D. W. Griffith's *A Corner in Wheat* (1909). The film tells three separate stories, intercutting images of a poor farm family, the "wheat king" who corners the market and thereby increases his fortune, and consumers in a bakery store, some of whom are unable to meet the rising price of bread. The characters from the three parallel plots never come into contact with one another in the film.

The wheat king makes his fortune and at the moment of triumph falls accidently to his death. The consumers face growing hardship as prices rise and the charity fund reduces its level of assistance. The farmer, who can show nothing for all his work, is left at the end of the film as he was found at the beginning, sowing seeds that offer little promise for his future. The film is structured so that the unifying theme—a progressive critique of capitalism—takes shape only in the minds of the viewers, who draw their own connections between the different parts of the story. Thus, the structure of the film keeps the message clear. If the three plots intersected more directly, or if characters were allowed to confront one another on the screen, the central philosophical message might have been muddled by the specifics of the stories or the characterizations.

Many films rely on symbols familiar from literature and theater to communicate ideas, for example, the candle that goes out on the table as an old man dies in bed. One of the most effective sequences in *The Return of Martin Guerre* deals with the impostor's first day in Artigat. At the end of the day Bertrande takes him to her bed, but first she is seen quickly removing the crucifix that has been left on her pillow. The meaning of the symbol is somewhat clouded because up to this point the film has led the audience to believe that the man is the real Martin Guerre. Once the audience realizes that he is an impostor, the significance of Bertrande removing the crucifix just before commiting what she must have considered the first of a series of mortal sins becomes more meaningful.

In the last two decades many film scholars have sought to study the making of meaning in film through an approach to linguistics known as semiology. Semiologists draw upon the work of linguist Ferdinand de Saussure, who defined a sign as made up of both the signifier (some visual element) and the signified (the concept or idea that the signifier stands for). A donkey, for example, can be signified by a drawing or by the letters d-o-n-k-e-y. In each case, a visual symbol (the signifier) stands for the meaning of a four-legged animal with long ears (the signified). The image of a donkey in a film carries with it the direct and overt denotative message: "Here is a four-legged animal with long ears." But it is the connotative meaning of visual images that makes film interesting. Semiotic analysis considers the additional connotative meanings that might be connected with the presence of the donkey, whether consciously intended by the filmmaker or unintentionally constructed in the mind of the viewer, and how that meaning is created. Typically, semiologists look for such meaning through analyses, which they term either paradigmatic (how this donkey is different from other donkeys or other animals that might have been shown) or syntagmatic (how this image of a donkey relates to the other images that precede or follow it within the film). The analysis would proceed through a careful categorization of possible denotative or connotative readings and a consideration of possible codes of meaning drawn from the broader culture, from other arts, or from the nature of the cinema.

Luis Bunuel's classic short film, *Un Chien Andalou* (1929), is a wonderful artifact for the study of surrealism and the intellectual history of the 1920s. From the opening sequence, which climaxes in the slicing of a woman's eye with a razor, *Un Chien Andalou* shocks its viewers with its destruction of contemporary aesthetic standards, thus accomplishing one of the central goals of surrealism as an artistic and intellectual movement. Many of the other images in the film have more or less obvious symbolic meaning. In one shot, a man, to approach a woman sexually, must drag behind him symbols of the repressive forces of bourgeois culture (a grand piano), organized religion (two priests), and moral corruption (the carcasses of two dead donkeys). The meaning of the donkeys in this image comes from the composition of the shot, which forces viewers to relate to the priests, the piano, and the donkeys at the same; from the half-decomposed state of the carcasses (a paradigmatic observation); and from the placement of the shot within in a film that dwells on the moral corruption of the main character (a syntagmatic observation).

Those who apply the theories of structuralism or semiology are sometimes faulted for taking their analyses too far. A thoroughgoing semiologist, for example, concentrating on the identification and de-coding of every sign, might fail to appreciate the aesthetic qualities of a film. Overly rigorous attention to the internal analysis of a moving-image production might lead scholars to undervalue, or even ignore, historical context. But historians concerned with the moving image cannot afford to turn their backs on film theory. The symbolic meaning in many film images might be discerned without necessarily resorting to the technical terminology of cinema theory, but there are surely occasions where a judicious application of such principles might offer new insight.

It is important to recognize that differences do exist in analyzing images in film and television. Television productions are almost always designed to fit more precise time limits than commercial entertainment films. Characteristically, television programs are also internally structured to allow for the insertion of commercials. A dramatic program is therefore likely to string out a series of mini-climaxes in such a way that the viewers' attention will be held until after the commercial break.

In addition, there are significant visual differences between film and television. The small TV screen does not lend itself to the vast panoramas and long shots that are so powerful in moving pictures, especially in Cinemascope and other wide-screen formats. Television footage, much more than film, involves head-and-shoulder shots of individual actors or small groups of actors. This was at least one reason why the makers of "Molders of Troy" decided to focus on the experience of one family, trying to represent the complex of worker, industry, and community history in the lives of a handful of people. There is also some degree of difference between the production techniques of film and television. While almost all of network television today is presented on videotape, only a small percentage (and a significantly larger percentage of local television) is broadcast live or almost live (taped earlier but shown as shot without editing). The typical sitcom, which may be carefully rehearsed and revised over several days, is usually shot as a run-through of the entire episode. This is very different from the shooting of a typical film or dramatic TV series, which is almost always shot with little, if any, attention to the order of the sequences as they will appear in the completed production.

There are many communications scholars who would argue that film and television are so unlike one another that they defy common treatment, but the interests of most history teachers should not demand such precision. There are distinctions between the content, production, and reception of the two media, but lessons should concentrate on the basic visual and aural elements that do raise similar, if not identical, analytical concerns.

FOR FURTHER READING

This book for teachers was prepared as part of a larger project funded by the National Endowment for the Humanities. The other elements to result from the project are the video compilation, which has been referred to throughout this discussion, and a book of essays to be entitled *Image as Artifact: The Historical Analysis of Film and Television*, in which twelve scholars concentrate on filling out the four frameworks for inquiry. Arrangements are not yet complete regarding the publication of *Image as Artifact*, but when it appears, it should prove especially helpful to teachers trying to apply the concepts proposed in this discussion.

The field of film and television scholarship has become so rich in the past decade that it would be impossible to adequately summarize it here. A few of the most influential publications in each area are listed on the following pages, but teachers are strongly encouraged to turn to the fuller bibliographies in James Monaco, *How To Read a Film*, rev. ed. (New York, 1981), and David Bordwell and Kristin Thompson, *Film Art: An Introduction*, 2d ed. (New York, 1986).

There are two journals that should be of special interest. *The Historical Journal of Film, Radio and Television* is published in Great Britain for the International Association for Audio-Visual Media in Historical Research and Teaching (IAMHIST). *Film & History* is the quarterly journal of the Historians Film Committee, an affiliated society of the American Historical Association based at New Jersey Institute of Technology, Newark, NJ 07102.

General Guides for Evaluating Films and Television

Blackaby, Linda, Dan Georgakas, and Barbara Margolis. *In Focus: A Guide to Using Films*. New York: Zoetrope, 1980.

Ferris, Bill, and Judy Peiser, eds. *American Folklore Films and Videotapes–An Index*. Memphis, Tenn.: Center for Southern Folklore, 1976.

Guidelines for Off-Air Taping of Copyrighted Programs for Education Use: Thirty Questions Librarians Ask. Chicago: American Library Association, 1982.

Klotman, Phyllis Rauch. *Frame By Frame: A Black Filmography*. Bloomington: Indiana University Press, 1979.

Limbacher, James L., comp. and ed. *Feature Films on 8-mm, 16-mm, and Videotape*. 7th ed. New York: Bowker, 1982.

Loy, Jane M. *Latin America, Sights and Sounds*. Gainesville, Fla.: Latin American Studies Programs, 1973.

Pettit, Arthur G. *Images of the Mexican American in Fiction and Film.* College Station, Texas: Texas A & M University Press, 1980.

Peyton, Patricia, ed. *Reel Change: A Guide to Social Issue Films.* San Francisco: Film Fund, 1979.

Pitts, Michael. *Hollywood and American Reality: A Filmography of Over 250 Motion Pictures Depicting U.S. History.* Jefferson, N.C.: McFarland, 1984.

Samples, Gordon. *How to Locate Reviews of Plays and Films: A Bibliography of Criticism from the Beginning to the Present.* Metuchen, N.J.: Scarecrow, 1976.

Sullivan, Kaye. *Films for, by, and about Women.* Metuchen, N.J.: Scarecrow, 1980.

Weatherford, Elizabeth, ed. *Native Americans on Film and Video.* New York: Museum of the American Indian, 1981.

Woll, Allen L., and Randall M. Miller. *Ethnic and Racial Images in American Film and Television: Historical Essays and Bibliography.* New York: Garland, 1987

Sources on Film

Aldgate, Anthony. *Cinema and History: British Newsreels and the Spanish Civil War.* London: Scholar Press, 1979.

Arnheim, Rudolf. *Film As Art.* Berkeley: University of California Press, 1957.

Balio, Tino. *United Artists: The Company Built by the Stars.* Madison: University of Wisconsin Press, 1976.

————, ed. *The American Film Industry.* Rev. ed. Madison: University of Wisconsin Press, 1985.

Barnouw, Erik. *Documentary: A History of the Non-Fiction Film.* New York: Oxford University Press, 1983.

Barsam, Richard Meran. *Non-Fiction Film: A Critical History.* New York: E. P. Dutton, 1973.

————, ed. *Non-Fiction Film Theory and Criticism.* New York: E. P. Dutton, 1976.

Bergman, Andrew. *We're in the Money: Depression America and its Films.* New York: New York University Press, 1971.

Bordwell, David, Janet Staiger, and Kristin Thompson. *The Classical Hollywood Cinema: Film Style and Mode of Production to 1960.* New York: Columbia University Press, 1985.

Burns, E. Bradford. *Latin American Cinema: Film and History.* Los Angeles: UCLA Latin American Center, 1975.

Cripps, Thomas. *Slow Fade to Black: The Negro in American Film, 1900-1942.* New York: Oxford University Press, 1977.

Fielding, Raymond. *A Technological History of Motion Pictures and Televison.* 3d ed. Berkeley: University of California Press, 1979.

————. *The American Newsreel, 1911-1967*. Norman: University of Oklahoma Press, 1972.

Gomery, Douglas, and Robert C. Allen. *Film History: Theory and Practice*. New York: Knopf, 1985.

Griffin, Patrick. "The Making of *Goodbye Billy*." *Film & History*, 2 (May 1972): 6-10.

Isaksson, Følke, and Leif Furhammar. *Politics and Film*. New York: Praeger, 1971.

Jarvie, Ian. *Movies and Society*. New York: Basic Books, 1970.

Jowett, Garth. *Film: The Democratic Art*. Boston: Little, Brown, 1976.

Jowett, Garth, and James M. Linton. *Movies as Mass Communication*. Beverly Hills: Sage, 1980.

Jowett, Garth, and Victoria O'Donnell. *Propaganda and Persuasion*. Newbury Park, Calif: Sage, 1986.

Kracauer, Siegfried. *From Caligari to Hitler: A Psychological History of the German Film*. Princeton: Princeton University Press, 1947.

Leab, Daniel J. *From Sambo to Superspade: The Black Motion Picture Experience*. Boston: Houghton Mifflin, 1975.

Maltby, Richard. *Harmless Entertainment: Hollywood and the Ideology of Consensus*. Metuchen, N.J.: Scarecrow, 1983.

Marsden, Michael, John G. Nachbar, and Sam L. Grogg, Jr., eds. *Movies as Artifacts: Cultural Criticism of Popular Film*. Chicago: Nelson-Hall, 1982.

Mast, Gerald, and Marshall Cohen. *Film Theory and Criticism: Introductory Readings*. 2d ed. New York: Oxford University Press, 1979.

Mast, Gerald, ed. *The Movies in Our Midst: Documents in the Cultural History of Film in America*. Chicago: University of Chicago Press, 1982.

May, Larry. *Screening Out the Past: The Birth of Mass Culture and the Motion Picture Industry*. New York: Oxford University Press, 1980.

Mellencamp, Patricia, and Philip Rosen. *Cinema Histories, Cinema Practices*. Frederick, Md.: University Publications of America, 1984.

O'Connor, John E., ed. *Film and the Humanities*. New York: Rockefeller Foundation, 1977.

Pronay, Nicholas, and Derek W. Spring. *Propaganda, Politics and Film, 1918-45*. London: Macmillan, 1982.

Reader, Keith. *Cultures on Celluloid*. London: Quartet Books, 1981.

Rollins, Peter C. "The Making of Will Rogers' 1920s." *Film & History*, 7 (January 1977): 1-5.

————, ed. *Hollywood as Historian: American Film in Cultural Context*. Lexington, Ky.: University Press of Kentucky, 1983.

Short, K. R. M., ed. *Film and Radio Propaganda in World War II.* Knoxville: University of Tennessee Press, 1983.

Smith, Julian. *Looking Away: Hollywood and Vietnam.* New York: Scribner, 1975.

Sklar, Robert. *Movie-Made America: A Cultural History of American Movies.* New York: Random House, 1975.

Suid, Lawrence. *Guts and Glory: Great American War Movies.* Reading, Mass.: Addison-Wesley, 1978.

Taylor, Richard. *The Politics of the Soviet Cinema, 1917-1929.* Cambridge, U.K.: Cambridge University Press, 1979.

Welch, David. *Propaganda and the German Cinema, 1933-1945.* New York: Oxford University Press, 1983.

Wollen, Peter. *Signs and Meaning in the Cinema.* Bloomington: Indiana University Press, 1969.

Wood, Michael. *America in the Movies.* New York: Basic Books, 1975.

Wright, Will. *Sixguns and Society: A Structural Study of the Western.* Berkeley: University of California Press, 1975.

Sources on Television

Adams, William, and Fay Schreibman, eds. *Television Network News: Issues in Content Research.* Washington, D.C.: George Washington Univerity, 1978.

Berger, Arthur Asa. *Media Analysis Techniques.* Beverly Hills: Sage, 1982.

Barnouw, Erik. *The Image Empire.* New York: Oxford University Press, 1970.

———. *Tube of Plenty.* New York: Oxford University Press, 1975.

———. *The Sponsor: Notes on a Modern Potentate.* New York: Oxford University Press, 1978.

Bergreen, Laurence. *Look Now, Pay Later: The Rise of Network Broadcasting.* Garden City, N.Y.: Doubleday, 1980.

Boorstin, Daniel. *The Image: Or, What Happened to the American Dream.* New York: Atheneum, 1962.

Brown, Les. *Television: The Business Behind the Box.* New York: Harcourt, Brace, and Jovanovich, 1971.

Chester, Edward W. *Radio, Television, and American Politics.* New York: Sheed and Ward Publishers, 1969.

Comstock, George, Steven Chaffee, Nathan Katzman, Maxwell McCombs, and Donald Roberts. *Television and Human Behavior.* New York: Columbia University Press, 1978

Diamond, Edwin, and Stephen Bates. *The Spot: The Rise of Political Advertising on Television.* Cambridge, Mass.: MIT Press, 1984.

Epstein, Edward Jay. *News From Nowhere: Television and the News.* New York: Random House, 1973.

Fiske, John. *Reading Television*. London: Methuen, 1978.

Gans, Herbert. *Deciding What's News*. New York: Pantheon, 1979.

Gitlin, Todd. *Inside Prime Time*. New York: Pantheon, 1983.

————, ed. *Watching Television*. New York: Pantheon, 1986.

Glasgow University Media Group. *Bad News*. Vol. I. London: Routledge & Kegal Paul, 1976.

Levinson, Richard, and William Link. *Stay Tuned: An Inside Look at the Making of Prime Time Television*. New York: St. Martin's, 1981.

MacDonald, J. Fred. *Television and the Red Menace: The Video Road to Vietnam*. New York: Praeger, 1985.

————. *Blacks and White TV: Afro-Americans in Television since 1948*. Chicago: Nelson Hall, 1983.

Mankiewicz, Frank, and Joel Swerdlow. *Remote Control: Television and the Manipulation of American Life*. New York: Times Books, 1978.

Marc, David. *Demographic Vistas: Television in American Culture*. Philadelphia: University of Pennsylvania Press, 1984.

Meyrowitz, Joshua. *No Sense of Place: The Impact of Electronic Media on Social Behavior*. New York: Oxford University Press, 1985.

Newcomb, Horace, ed. *Television: The Critical View*. 4th ed. New York: Oxford University Press, 1987.

Postman, Neil V. *Amusing Ourselves to Death: Public Discourse in the Age of Show Business*. New York: Viking, 1985.

Ranney, Austin. *Channels of Power: The Impact of Television on American Politics*. New York: Basic Books, 1983.

Robinson, John P., and Mark R. Levy. *The Main Source: Learning From Television News*. Beverly Hills: Sage, 1986.

Rollins, Peter C. "Television's Vietnam: The Visual Language of Television News." *Journal of American Culture*, 4 (Summer 1981): 114-35.

Sklar, Robert. *Prime-time America: Life On and Behind the Television Screen*. New York: Oxford University Press, 1980.

Westin, Av. *Newswatch: How TV Decides the News*. New York: Simon and Schuster, 1982.

Williams, Raymond. *Television: Technology and Cultural Form*. New York: Schoken, 1975

Sources on the Connections Between History and the Moving Image

Abrash, Barbara, and Janet Sternberg, eds. *Historians & Filmmakers: Toward Collaboration*. New York: The Institute for Research in History, 1983.

Burns, E. Bradford. "Conceptualizing the Use of Film to Study History." *Film & History*, 4 (December 1974): 1-11.

Ferro, Marc. "1917: History and Cinema." *Contemporary History*, 3 (October 1968): 45-61.

Fledelius, Karsten, Kaare Rübner Jorgenson, Niels Skyum-Nielson, and Erik H. Swiatek. *Studies in History, Film and Society I: History and the Audio-Visual Media.* Copenhagen: Eventus, 1979.

Leab, Daniel J. "Writing History With Film: Two Views of the 1937 Strike Against General Motors by the UAW." *Labor History*, 21 (Winter 1979-80): 102-12.

O'Connor, John E., and Martin A. Jackson., eds. *American History/ American Film: Interpreting the Hollywood Image.* New York: Ungar, 1979.

O'Connor, John E., ed. *American History/American Television: Interpreting the Video Past.* New York: Ungar, 1983.

Pronay, Nicholas, Betty R. Smith, and Tom Hastie. *The Use of Film in History Teaching.* London: Historical Association, 1972.

Raack, Richard C. "Clio's Dark Mirror: The Documentary Film in History," *History Teacher*, 6 (1972): 109-18.

————. "Historiography and Cinematography: A Prolegomenon to Film Work for Historians." *Journal of Contemporary History*, 18 (July 1983): 411-38.

Reimers, K. F., and H. Friedrich, eds. *Studies in History, Film and Society III: Contemporary History in Film and Television.* Munich: Verlagölschläger, 1982.

Short, K. R .M., and Karsten Fledelius, eds. *Studies in History, Film and Society II: History and Film: Methodology, Research, Education.* Copenhagen: Eventus, 1980.

Short, K. R. M., ed. *Feature Films as History.* Knoxville: University of Tennessee Press, 1981.

Smith, Paul, ed. *The Historian and Film.* Cambridge, U.K.: Cambridge University Press, 1976.

Sorlin, Pierre. *The Film in History.* Totowa, N.J.: Barnes and Noble, 1980.

Toplin, Robert Brent. "The Making of Denmark Vesey's Rebellion." *Film & History*, 12 (September 1982): 49-56.

Walkowitz, Daniel. "Visual History: The Craft of the Historian Filmmaker." *Public Historian*, 7 (Winter 1985): 53-64.

APPENDIX A

Sample Class Assignment

Your assignment involves an analysis of *The Plow That Broke the Plains* (1936). This U.S. government-produced documentary film focuses on the problems of the dust bowl of the thirties and, by tracing the history of the settlement and development of the region, seeks to explain how humans contributed to environmental tragedy.

Your paper should concentrate on one of the seven major sequences of the film (as screened and discussed in class):

- "Prologue"

- "Settlement"

- "Warning"

- "Wheat Will Win the War"

- "Twenties Boom"

- "Dust Bowl"

- "Migration"

Using at least three of the historical sources from the bibliography provided, analyze and evaluate the interpretation presented by the film. How well does the film present the facts of the situation? How does its interpretation of issues and events fit into the view offered by the literature, then and now?

Include in your analysis specific reference to at least three shots and two editing transitions from the sequence chosen that, to your mind, contribute significantly to the message of the film. Consider how the information and point of view offered by the film is supported (or not supported) by the visual and aural elements contained in them. To help you focus on these shots and transitions in detail, fill out one of the Shot Analysis sheets and one of the Editing Analysis sheets for each and submit them with your paper.

Papers should be five to six pages (typed, double-spaced), plus citations, bibliography, three Shot Analysis sheets, and two Editing Analysis sheets.

Shot Analysis

1. Sketch the image as it appears on the screen. Use more than one sketch if camera movement significantly alters the composition of the shot. Use the back of the page if you need to make more than two sketches.

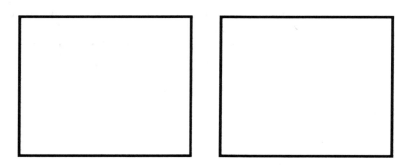

2. In one sentence, describe each of the following elements of the shot and, if applicable, the way it contributes to the meaning of the shot:

   - duration
   - lighting
   - color
   - field size
   - composition
   - camera angle
   - camera movement
   - focus
   - lens characteristics
   - projection speed

3. Is the shot, in your view, primarily denotative or connotative? Explain. If it is both, explain how it functions in each way.

4. What codes are operative? Are they primarily cultural or cinematic? Explain.

5. How does the sound track (narration, music, sound effects, etc.) contribute to the message of the shot?

6. Explain in your own words how this shot contributes to the point the filmmaker is trying to make in the sequence of which it is a part.

Editing Analysis

1. Sketch each of the shots connected by the edit in question.

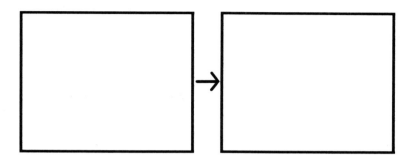

2. Identify the type of editing device used (is it a slow dissolve, fast dissolve, jump cut, match cut, etc.).

3. Explain how the sound track influences the association of the two shots.

4. Describe in your own words how the association of these two shots contributes to the point the filmmaker is trying to make in the sequence in question.

APPENDIX B

Video Compilation

Selection 1. *The Return of Martin Guerre* (excerpts)

Selection 2. "Molders of Troy" (excerpt)

Selection 3. *Women of Summer* (excerpt)

Selection 4. The Cutaway and the Editing of a Television News Interview

Selection 5. *The Plow That Broke the Plains*

Selection 6. The "Daisy Spot"

Selection 7. Universal and Movietone Newsreels (excerpts)

Selection 8. "See It Now: Report on Senator McCarthy" (excerpts)

Selection 9. CBS Evening News, December 2, 1979 (excerpt)

Selection 10. *The Birth of a Race* (excerpts)

Selection 11. *Für Uns*

Selection 12. *Life of an American Fireman* (excerpts)

Selection 13. *A Corner in Wheat*

DCP1M2/9